MERLIN'S PUZZLE PASTIMES

Edited by Charles Barry Townsend

DOVER PUBLICATIONS, INC., NEW YORK

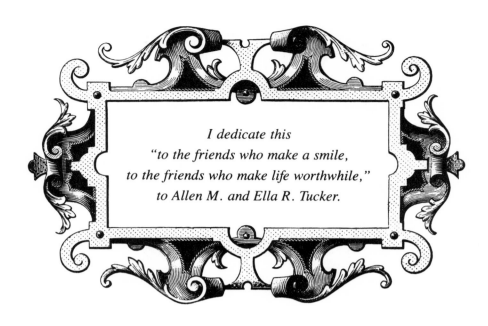

I dedicate this
"to the friends who make a smile,
to the friends who make life worthwhile,"
to Allen M. and Ella R. Tucker.

Copyright © 1976, 1977 and 1979 by Hammond Incorporated.
Copyright © 1986 by Charles Barry Townsend.
All rights reserved under Pan American and International Copyright Conventions.

Published in Canada by General Publishing Company, Ltd., 30 Lesmill Road, Don Mills, Toronto, Ontario.
Published in the United Kingdom by Constable and Company, Ltd.

This Dover edition, first published in 1986, contains 53 puzzle pages and the corresponding solutions selected from *Merlin's Puzzler* (1976; apparently originally issued as *Merlin's Scrapbook*), *Merlin's Puzzler Volume 2* (1977), and *Merlin's Puzzler Volume 3* (1979), originally published by Hammond Incorporated, Maplewood, N.J.

Manufactured in the United States of America
Dover Publications, Inc., 31 East 2nd Street, Mineola, N.Y. 11501

Library of Congress Cataloging-in-Publication Data

Townsend, Charles Barry.
  Merlin's puzzle pastimes.

  Selected puzzles and solutions from the author's Merlin's puzzler. 1976–1979.
  Summary: A collection of puzzles, riddles, and problems selected by the author from his earlier volumes.
  1. Puzzles—Juvenile literature. 2. Riddles—Juvenile literature. [1. Puzzles. 2. Riddles] I. Title.
GV1493.T6825   1986   793.93   86-4389
ISBN 0-486-25123-3

rthur's Castle, The Knights of The Round Table, Camelot, Merlin, Lancelot, Guinevere. These places and people conjure up in our minds visions of great events, daring deeds and subtle intrigue. A whole, rich world alive and vibrant which seems as real to us today as it was 1,400 years ago. Or was it real? Did it all really happen? It is said that when the end came to Camelot and Arthur's dream was shattered, his adviser Merlin, saddened by the knowledge that even his vast powers were unable to help Arthur in his hour of greatest need, retreated to a place called the "Isle of Merlin." Today the Isle of Merlin, like the Scottish village of Brigadoon, exists only in time and space. The Isle of Merlin is inhabited by people and animals. It has both farms and cities, rivers and mountains. It is great and it is small and completely without precedent. Merlin and his Isle are able to travel through time visiting both the past and the future. It was while visiting the present and seeing the current interest in the Arthurian legend that Merlin decided to make available for publication his notes concerning some of the great interests of his life, namely puzzles, games and magic. This volume constitutes a broad selection of the best puzzles, games and magic that have amused and entertained the world since the dawn of recorded history.

Quantity is not the emphasis here, but rather quality. We want to preserve in one set of writings the very best example of these arts. Merlin also feels that these secrets are deserving of better illustrations than have formerly been accorded to books of this nature. To this end your editor has drawn heavily on the works of the master engravers of the past to help in the graphic presentation of Merlin's problems.

That completes my introduction to this volume of Merlin's puzzles. I have had a grand time putting it all together and I am confident that you will enjoy the challenges propounded by Merlin. Happy puzzling to you!

Your Editor,

Charles Barry Townsend

The Man In The Iron Mask

When the three musketeers broke into the dungeon beneath the Bastille, they found not one man in an iron mask but five. Which one was the true king of France? By asking the guard some quick questions they learned the fourteen facts I have listed below. Coupled with the knowledge that the true king of France drank only wine, they were able to discover which prisoner to free. Can you do it, too? Hurry up, I hear more guards coming.

(1) The man in the red mask has a cell with a stone door.
(2) The man in the green mask wears sandals.
(3) Tea is drunk in the cell with the oak door.
(4) The man in the blue mask drinks water.
(5) The cell with the oak door is to the right (your right) of the cell with the barred door.
(6) The man who eats chicken wears boots.
(7) Beef is eaten in the cell with the iron door.
(8) Beer is drunk in the middle cell.
(9) The man in the black mask has the first cell on the left.
(10) The man who eats fish lives next to the man who wears shoes.
(11) Beef is eaten in the cell next to the man who wears only socks.
(12) The man who eats pies drinks milk.
(13) The man in the yellow mask eats grapes.
(14) The man in the black mask is in the cell next to the one with the paneled door.

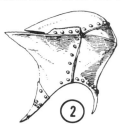

① ② ③ ④ ⑤

THE FESTIVAL OF PUZZLES

I t's festival time once again on the Isle of Merlin. The puzzle experts from all parts of the island are converging on the capital. In the press release picture on the next page we see Merlin arriving aboard his flagship, *Merlin 1*. The city is decked out with puzzles on the buildings, bridges and airships. Let's move in for a closer look at some of the more outstanding problems.

High atop one of the twin towers in front of Merlin's ship they have erected a new television antenna (1). The instructions in the festival's convention catalogue read as follows: "The design of this antenna can be drawn using one continuous line and without any line crossing any other line." That should keep the contestants busy for a while.

The office personnel on the other twin tower came up with an equally interesting problem (2). They have hung the numerals 1, 6 and 3 on the outside of their building. "You are to arrange these numbers into one number that can be evenly divided by seven." Merlin particularly likes the ingenious solution to this puzzle.

Hanging on the Park Plaza office building is the face of a gigantic six-sided clock (3). "The puzzler may run out of time attempting to solve this puzzle. The challenge is simple. Merely rearrange the numbers on the clock so that the sum of each of the six sides totals 17."

Moving down the picture we find that the bridge workers have put up a giant Tinker Toy-like structure on top of one end of the King Arthur Bridge (4). Our guidebook reads, "This toy-like structure is composed of 9 equal-size triangles. By removing 5 of the girders reduce the number to 5 equal-size triangles."

To the left of the bridge, painted on the top side of the giant passenger dirigible (5), is an Indian puzzle. "Take the four Indian arrowheads and arrange them in such a way as to have five arrowheads."

Finally, Merlin noted from his airship that nine of his escort balloons were flying in such a formation that there were 3 rows with 4 balloons in each row. Some of the balloons, of course, were in more than one row. "I'll have to add this puzzle to the convention's itinerary," thought Merlin.

Well, readers, there are some of the festival problems for this year. Come along now and join the fun. The shuttle dirigible for the Park Plaza is leaving in five minutes.

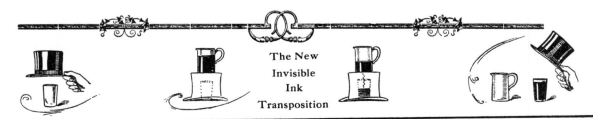

The New Invisible Ink Transposition

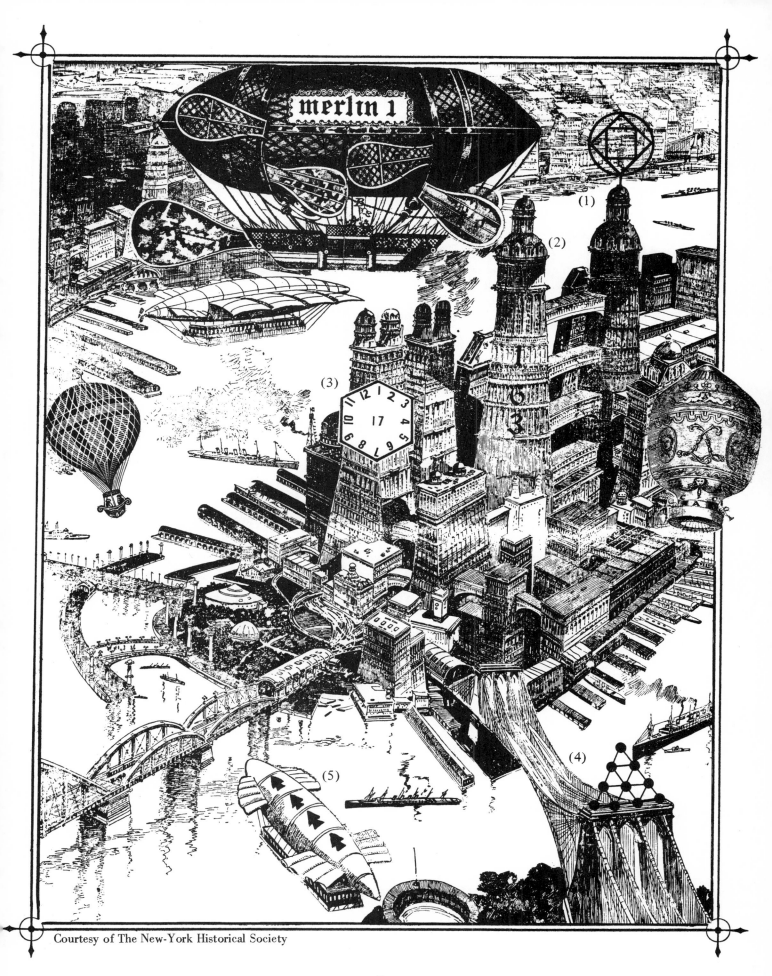

merlin 1

Merlin's Notes

Flash Farrington, Merlin's court photographer, sent over to your editor the other day three photographs illustrating some scenes from last year's puzzle convention. The puzzle convention, you may recall, was held in Merlin's Crystal Palace on the other side of the island. Merlin has promised me that during our stay here he will take us to this year's convention.

The first photograph shows the boys from one of the local puzzle clubs rolling a drum up to the judges' platform. Painted on the end of the drum is a puzzle in flatland design. You are to discern how many continuous strokes are required to draw this design. You may not lift your pencil from the paper while drawing it. Every time your pencil changes direction it is to be considered a new stroke. You will have to draw over the same line more than once to solve it. What is the smallest number of strokes needed to duplicate the design?

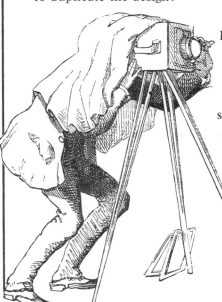

The second photo depicts the layout of a famous old English garden "maze." It is not a difficult maze, but I am sure that you will enjoy finding your way to the center of it.

Now look at the puzzle held by the gentleman in picture 3. Can you draw one continuous line that crosses every line once, and only once? Fig. 1 shows how this can be done by going "over" a line without crossing it, but another solution fulfills the conditions perfectly. If you can figure it out, we will consider you a master puzzler. Editor's hint: Draw the figure on a donut. That's a hint?

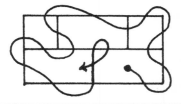

Fig. 1

The Pharaoh's Curse

When the tomb of the Egyptian Pharaoh Riddles the IV was opened it was found to be guarded by the triple curse of Thoth. Whoever gazes upon the resting place of the pharaoh (and that now includes you since by this time you have looked at the drawing on the next page) must correctly answer the following three questions. If you fail to answer all of them you may be in for a visit from Anubis, guardian of the netherworld.

Question 1 – The problem is to place eleven coins on the black dots which encircle the shield of Hammurabi. Starting at any dot, count six sixth dot. Continue this on different dots. a coin on it is dot and counted

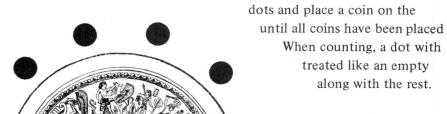 

dots and place a coin on the until all coins have been placed When counting, a dot with treated like an empty along with the rest.

Question 2 – This question is very easy. How many triangles are there in the figure below?

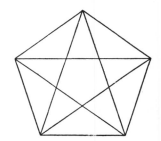

Question 3 – Using the numbered diagram at the bottom of the page, place four dimes and four pennies on squares one through eight. Alternate the coins: dime, penny, dime, penny, as shown in Figure 1.

Fig. 1 ⬜⚫⬜⚫⬜⚫⬜⚫⬜⬜

When the coins have been set up, move them, two at a time, so that after four moves they are positioned as shown in Figure 2.

Fig. 2 ⬜⬜⚫⚫⚫⚫⬜⬜⬜⬜

1	2	3	4	5	6	7	8	9	10

hile browsing in a used book store I came upon an interesting old copy of a Funk and Wagnalls Dictionary from 1915. Below is a list of 18 words from it. Can you match 12 of them to the pictures I've used to make up a sample page from this old tome?

(A) Stereoscope

(B) Parbuckle

(C) Catalo

(D) Xat

(E) Fiacre

(F) Adjutant

(G) Char-a-banc

(H) Ballista

(I) Bark

(J) Cutter

(K) Juggernaut

(L) Peccary

(M) Bittern

(N) Uhlan

(O) Coot

(P) Sphygmograph

(Q) Cowl

(R) Roentgen Rays

hat we are looking at is truly a frightening picture from the past. The palace is that of Sennacherib at Kouyunjik. An evil Jinn is materializing behind the palace, and it will soon command Sennacherib to solve the Pyramid Puzzle of Ur or face destruction. To work this puzzle, you must first place fourteen coins on all the circles of the pyramid except circle 6. Then jumping one coin over another, as you would in checkers and removing the jumped checker, you try to remove every coin from the board except one. You can only jump along the diagonal lines and the lines across the bottom row.

Can you save the palace from certain destruction? Hurry, there is not much more time to save them!

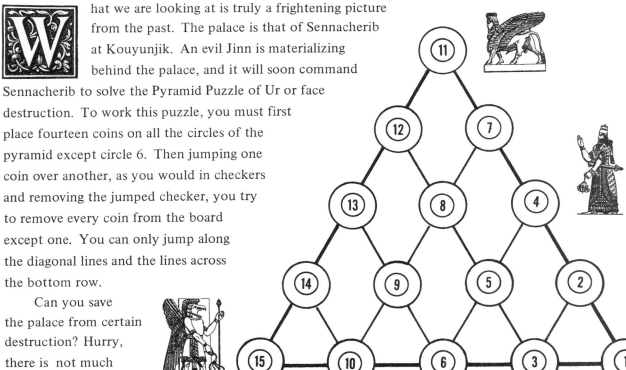

The Black Widow

Professor Pepper has graciously consented to exhibit once again his famous illusion, the Black Widow. The Widow has a choice selection of riddles to ensnare your wits in a web of confusion. Professor, awaken the little lady, her victims . . . 'er I should say, her audience is ready and waiting!

(1) When the clock strikes thirteen, what time is it?

(2) In what month do girls talk the least?

(3) How many balls of twine would it take to reach to the moon?

(4) Who was the greatest actor in the Bible?

(5) What key is the hardest to turn?

(6) What goes up and never goes down?

(7) What has eighteen legs and catches flies?

(8) What is the difference between an elephant and a flea?

(9) When is butter like Irish children?

(10) When is a door not a door?

(11) What is the highest public building in your city?

(12) What is that which every living person has seen, but will never see again?

(13) What is the last thing you take off before going to bed?

(14) When was beef the highest that it has ever been?

(15) When does a public speaker steal lumber?

(16) Why is a ship the most polite thing in the world?

(17) What must one do to have soft hands?

(18) Where can happiness always be found?

Mr. Sherlock Holmes

"There, Watson, is the most dangerous woman in London today." "What, Mlle. Aimée? Surely you're joking, Holmes!" "I have every reason to believe that she was the one who broke into the Albert Museum last night and stole the Diamond of Calicut. Look at this diagram, Watson. Someone gained entrance here, at point <u>A</u>, by using an air vent located one foot below the ceiling and midway between the two sidewalls. He then made his way across the room to point <u>B</u>, where the diamond is stored in a wall safe built one foot above the floor and also midway between the sidewalls. As the entire floor, up to eight feet in front of the safe, is wired to an alarm system, the culprit could only have stolen the diamond by walking across the walls and ceiling and part of the floor. Taking into consideration the dimensions of the room, 30 feet long, by 12 feet wide, by 12 feet

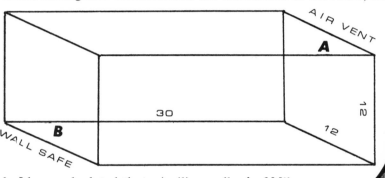

high, I have calculated that a 'ceiling walker' of Mlle. Aimée's skill and speed could have gotten from the vent to the safe, opened it and returned to the vent in the time between the security guards' rounds only if she could have plotted a route across the ceiling and walls that would have been exactly 40 feet in length."

"An interesting problem in geometry, Holmes, but I think that you're wrong. She's much too pretty to be a criminal!"

"Watson, you leave me speechless!"

Can you find the 40-foot route that the thief took?

"AIMÉE," THE HUMAN FLY.

rofessor Hoffmann wrote many books dealing with magic, puzzles and home entertainment in the latter part of the 19th and early 20th centuries. His outstanding work was *Modern Magic*. There is great charm and ease of manner in his style of writing which creates a lasting friendship between reader and author. My favorite selection is *Puzzles Old and New*, which runs to 394 pages of the most varied and excellent material. I have selected my favorite puzzles from this great book, along with many of the fine illustrations to be found therein. On the next 8 pages you will have the treat of matching wits with the good professor.

Good luck, my friends, the professor is a hard man to beat.

THE "ENGLISH SIXTEEN" PUZZLE

A clever puzzle, under the above title, is issued by Messrs. Heywood, of Manchester.

A board, as illustrated on the next page, is used, with eight white and eight red counters. These are arranged on the black squares, the red to the right, the white to the left, the central square, No. 9 in the drawing, being left vacant. The problem is to transpose the red and white counters, the men to be moved according to "draughts" rules — i.e., forward only; the whites towards the spaces occupied by the reds, and the reds towards the spaces occupied by the whites. The men move only on the black squares, and therefore diagonally. A white man can pass over a red man, or a red man over a white man, provided that the space next beyond is vacant.

A SINGULAR SUBTRACTION

Required, to subtract 45 from 45 in such manner that there shall be 45 left.

A MYSTERIOUS MULTIPLICAND

Required, to find a number which, multiplied by 3, 6, 9, 12, 15, 18, 21, 24, or 27, shall in each case give as the product the same digit, three times repeated.

AN UNMANAGEABLE LEGACY

An old farmer left a will whereby he bequeathed his horses to his three sons, John, James and William, in the following proportions: John, the eldest, was to have one-half, James to have one-third, and William one-ninth. When he died, however, it was found that the number of horses in his stable was seventeen, a number which is divisible neither by two, by three, or nine. In their perplexity the three brothers consulted a clever lawyer, who hit on a scheme whereby the intentions of the testator were carried out to the satisfaction of all parties.

How was it managed?

A NOVEL CENTURY

Required, by multiplication and addition of the numbers 1 to 9 inclusive, to make 100, each number being used once, and once only.

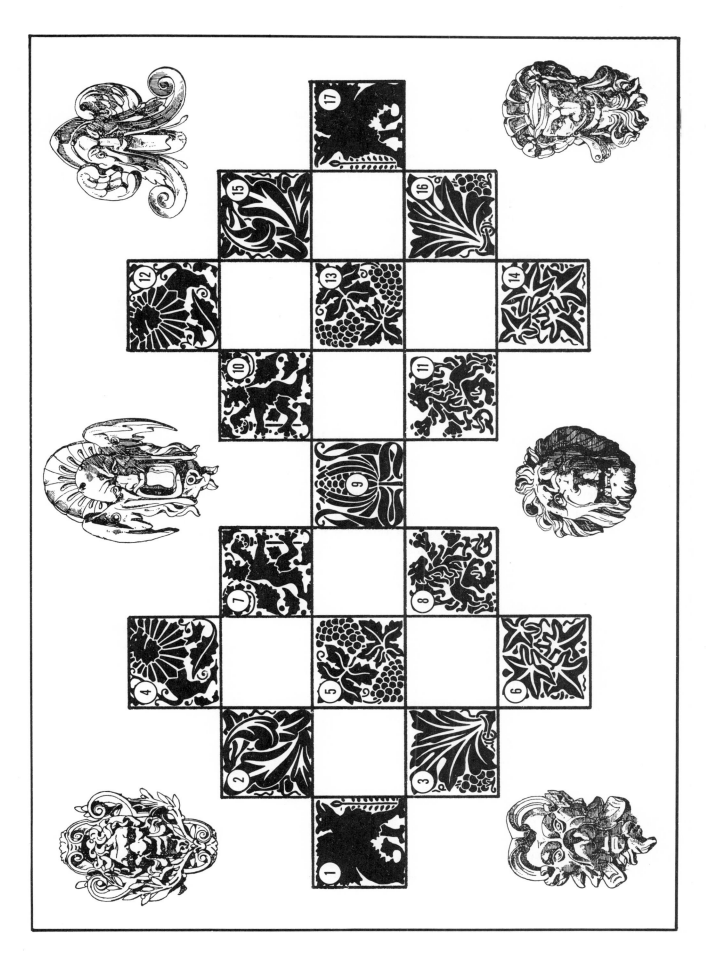

he following puzzles may be as hard to solve as getting loose from a Chinese Magic handcuff.

THE "TWENTY-SIX" PUZZLE

This is a magic square with a difference, the four corner places being omitted. The problem is to arrange the numbers 1 to 12 inclusive in the form of a cross, as shown in Fig. 1, so as to make 26 in seven different ways — viz., the two horizontal and the two vertical rows, the group of squares marked aaaa, the group marked bbbb, and group marked cccc, each making the above-mentioned total.

	b	b	
a	c	c	a
a	c	c	a
	b	b	

Fig. 1

MANY FIGURES, BUT A SMALL RESULT

Required, of the numbers 1, 2, 3, 4, 5, 6, 7, 8, 9, 0, to compose two fractions, whose sum shall be equal to 1. Each number to be used once, and once only.

THE CAPTIVES IN THE TOWER

An elderly queen, her daughter, and little son, weighing 195 pounds, 105 pounds, and 90 pounds respectively, were kept prisoners at the top of a high tower. The only communication with the ground below was a cord passing over a pulley, with a basket at each end, and so arranged that when one basket rested on the ground the other was opposite the window. Naturally, if the one were more heavily loaded than the other, the heavier would descend; but if the excess on either side was more than 15 pounds, the descent became so rapid as to be dangerous, and from the position of the rope the captives could not check it with their hands. The only thing available to help them in the tower was a cannonball, weighing 75 pounds. They, notwithstanding, contrived to escape.

How did they manage it?

A DIFFICULT DIVISION

A wine merchant has in his cellar 21 casks. Seven are full of wine; seven half-full, and seven empty.

How can he divide them (without transferring any portion of the liquid from cask to cask) among his three sons — Dick, Tom, and Harry — so that each shall have not only an equal quantity of wine, but an equal number of casks?

NOTHING LEFT

There is a certain number from which, if you subtract ten, multiply the remainder by three, find the square root of the product, and from such square root subtract eighteen, nothing is left. What is the number?

ore puzzles from the pen of Professor Hoffmann.

A PUZZLING INSCRIPTION

The following interesting inscription is said to be found in the chancel of a small church in Wales, just over the Ten Commandments. The addition of a single letter, repeated at various intervals, renders it not only intelligible, but appropriate to the situation:

P R S V R Y P R F C T M N

V R K P T H S P R C P T S T N

What is the missing letter?

DROPPED-LETTER PROVERBS

Supply the missing letters, and each of the series following will be found to represent a popular proverb. Each dash represents either a dropped letter or the space between two words. In some of the examples one dash stands for two dropped letters.

1) F-i-t-h-a-t-e-e-w-n-a-r-a-y.
2) B-r-s-f-f-t-r-f-c-t-g-t-r.
3) H-w-o-g-s-b-r-w-g-g-s-s-r-w-g.
4) T-k-c-r-f-h-p-n-n-t-e-p-n-s-w-l-t-k-c-r-f-t-e-s-l-s.

A PUZZLE WITH COINS

Required, to arrange twelve coins in such manner that they shall count four in a straight line in seven different directions.

A BRIDGE PROBLEM

With three wine glasses and three matches you are to form a bridge between the three wine glasses, using the matches, that will be strong enough to support a fourth wine glass.

Each match must rest on one glass only, and touch such glass only at a single point.

A SQUARE PUZZLE

You are to arrange four and twenty matches on a table so as to form nine squares as in Fig. 1.

Fig. 1

Required, to take away eight matches and leave two squares only.

SIX INTO THREE

Seventeen matches being laid on the table so as to form six equal squares as in Fig. 1, required, by taking away five matches, to leave three squares only.

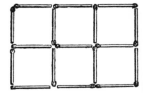
Fig. 1

SIX INTO TWO

Seventeen matches being laid on the table so as to form six equal squares (see Fig. 1), required, by taking away six matches, to leave two squares only.

FIVE INTO THREE

Fifteen matches being laid on the table so as to form five equal squares as in Fig. 2, required, by taking away three matches, to leave three squares only.

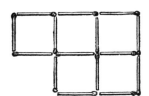
Fig. 2

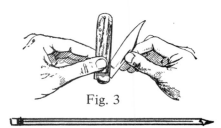
Fig. 3

THE BALANCED PENCIL

Given, a lead pencil, and a penknife (Fig. 3), with which you sharpen the pencil to the finest possible point.

Required, to balance the pencil in an upright, or nearly upright, position on the tip of the forefinger.

THE CUT PLAYING CARD

Given, a playing card or an oblong piece of cardboard of corresponding size.

Required, so to cut it, still keeping it in one piece, that a person of ordinary stature may be able to pass through it.

THE BALANCED QUARTER

The requirements for this puzzle are an ordinary paper clip, a hatpin or long sharpened pencil, a quarter, and a finger ring, about equal in weight to the quarter.

You are required, by the aid of the other two articles, to balance the quarter on the point of the pin or pencil.

WATER BEWITCHED

Required, to place a glass of water in such a position that the glass cannot be lifted without spilling the whole of the water.

The plain frame and handkerchief   Frame is covered and placed in a bag   Anything will pass through   Yet handkerchief is undisturbed

PASSING THE GATE

It was the rule in a certain continental town that anyone passing through either of the four city gates, whether going out or coming in, should pay a penny. A stranger arrived one day at the town, paid his penny and passed through the first gate. He spent in the town one-half of the money he had left and then went out again by the same gate, again paying a penny. The next day he did the like, entering and passing out by the second gate and meanwhile spending half his available cash in the town. On the following two days he did the same, entering and leaving by the third and fourth gates respectively. When he left the town for the fourth time he had only one penny left.

How much had he at first?

A FEAT OF DIVINATION

A couple of dice are thrown. The thrower is invited to double the points of one of the dice (whichever he pleases), add 5 to the result, multiply by 5 and add the points of the second die. He states the total, at which point anyone knowing the secret can instantly name the points of the two dice.

How is it done?

HIDDEN PROVERBS

The apparent jumble of letters in the figure below contains five well-known proverbs arranged in a systematic order. When the clue is once discovered, the proverbs can be read without difficulty.

PUZZLE: To find the five proverbs.

```
R E N O W N E D T H A N W
S Y O U R C A K E A N D A
S T E T O B E F E A R H R
E A R K S S P O I L E A F
L E O O H E R S N T D V O
O T M O T L I N O H T E U
N O S C A L A G M E H I R
S N I Y G O R S O B A T S
E N G N E N O T S R N P A
I A O A M O O T S O A E W
R C D E V I L A H T D A S
O U O Y N O I L D A E C A
T C I V R E H H T A H E Z
```

he "Forty-Five" Puzzle

The number 45 has some curious properties. Among others, it may be divided into four parts, in such manner that if you add two to the first, subtract two from the second, multiply the third by two, and divide the fourth by two, the result will in each case be equal. What are the results?

Squares, Product, and Difference

Required, to find two numbers the sum of whose squares is greater by 181 than their product, and whose product is greater by 161 than their difference.

The Two Ages

Father and son are aged 71 and 34 respectively. At what age was the father three times the age of his son; and at what age will the latter have reached half his father's age?

The Shepherd and His Sheep

A shepherd was asked how many sheep he had in his flock. He replied that he could not say, but he knew if he counted them by twos, by threes, by fours, by fives, or by sixes, there was always one over; but if he counted them by sevens, there was none over. What is the smallest number which will answer the above conditions?

When Will They Get It?

Seven guests at a restaurant came, the first every day, the second every other day, the third every third day, and so on to the seventh, who came once a week only. The host, in a liberal mood, declared that on the first day all came together he would treat them to a dinner gratis. How soon, according to the above order of rotation, would they be in position to claim his promise?

The Two Sons

An elderly mathematician was asked what were the ages of his two sons. He replied, "The one is five and a quarter years older than the other, and six times the age of the elder, added to five times the age of the younger, would be 301."

What was the age of each?

THE THIRTY-SIX PUZZLE

his is the last puzzle from Professor Hoffmann, so give it a good try.

Thirty-six counters are arranged in the form of a square, six rows of six each. Required, to remove six counters in such manner that the remaining counters shall still have an even number in each row, horizontal and vertical.

L'ENVOI

In the manner of Professor Hoffmann we would like to leave the readers with a short postscript. The Professor has once again reached across the borders of time and has entertained the readers of today with the charm and ingenuity of the puzzles of yesterday. For us, these puzzles are truly old wine in new bottles.

Thank you, Professor, for a most pleasant interlude.

Your Editor.

PROFESSOR HOFFMANN

 ards and conjuring have always gone together, as have cards and puzzles. Merlin has requested the prestidigitator above to entertain us with some puzzles and pasteboard statistics.

"Ladies and gentlemen, please take note that this innocent pack of playing cards that I hold in my hand is in reality a most ingenious form of calendar. Please note the following similarities:

(1) There are 52 playing cards and 52 weeks in the year.

(2) There are 13 cards in each suit and 13 weeks in each season.

(3) There are 4 suits and 4 seasons.

(4) There are 12 court (face) cards and 12 months in the year.

(5) The Red cards stand for day and the Black cards for night.

(6) If you total up the values of all the cards, counting Jacks as 11, Queens as 12, and Kings as 13, the sum will be 364. Add 1 to this for the Joker and you have the number of days in a year.

(7) Also of interest is the fact that if you add up all the letters in all the names of the cards, to wit: one, two, three, four, five, six, seven, eight, nine, ten, Jack, Queen, and King, you will get a total of 52, the number of cards in a deck of playing cards.

"Do you find these statistics a bit strange and disturbing? Is it mere coincidence, or is there something to the old admonition that a deck of cards is the Devil's picture book?"

THE ELEVEN TRICK

Tell your friends that you are about to show them a trick based on lightning calculation on your part. Discarding all of the face cards from the pack, take the remaining cards and start laying them down on the table in groups of three. Explain to your audience that each group of three cards forms a three-digit number that can be exactly divided by 11 without leaving a remainder. You form these three-digit numbers as fast as you can lay the cards down.

In our example we have formed the number 231. Eleven goes into this number exactly 21 times.

The explanation as to how the trick is performed is very simple. Just make sure that the total of the first card plus the third card adds up to the value of the middle card.

Simple . . . . . . but very, very good!

NO TWO IN THE SAME ROW

Fig. 1

Arrange the twelve court cards and the four aces into four rows of four cards each (something similar to Fig. 1). Now move the cards around until they are in such order that no two cards of the same suit or of the same value will be found in any row of four cards—either horizontally or vertically. This is a famous old card puzzle and is still one of the best.

THINGS ARE LOOKING UP!

Lay three cards on the table, two cards face-down and one card face-up (see Fig. 2). Now, in three moves, turning over two cards during each move, end up with all three cards facing upwards on the table.

This trick is sometimes performed with water glasses or coins, the answer being the same in all cases.

Fig. 2

THE FIVE PAIRS PUZZLE

Lay out a row of ten cards on the table. Starting with any card, pick it up and move it left or right over the next two cards in the row and place it on top of the third card. You now have a pair. Next, pick up another single card and pass it left or right over the next two cards in the row (a pair counts as one card), and place it on the third single card. You are to continue in this manner until you have five pairs upon the table.

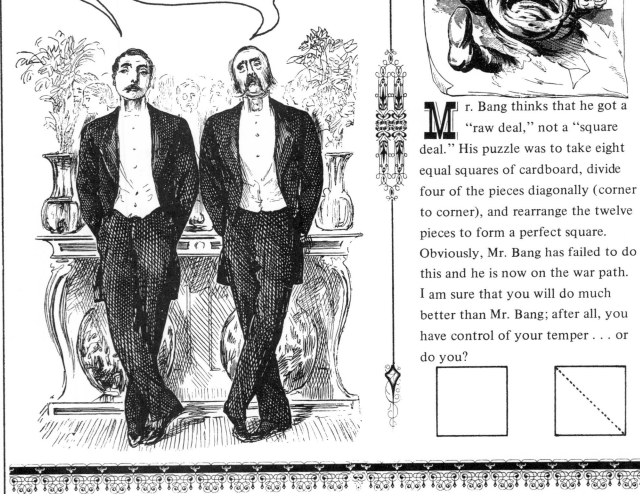

All right, Bertie, try this riddle on for size: What is it (you may not ask whether it is an animal, a bird or a reptile) that has this peculiarity — one leg cannot be raised from the ground without raising two or more legs?

That is a rum riddle, Clive, I'm dashed if I have the foggiest!

"A SQUARE DEAL FOR MR. BANG"

Mr. Bang thinks that he got a "raw deal," not a "square deal." His puzzle was to take eight equal squares of cardboard, divide four of the pieces diagonally (corner to corner), and rearrange the twelve pieces to form a perfect square. Obviously, Mr. Bang has failed to do this and he is now on the war path. I am sure that you will do much better than Mr. Bang; after all, you have control of your temper . . . or do you?

All right, quiet down over there. The Meeting of the Merlin Chapter of the Baker Street Irregulars is now in session. The first order of business is a new test that we have devised for evaluating the observational qualities of all new candidates for membership. I have here a detailed floor plan of Mr. Sherlock Holmes's flat in Baker Street. The applicant will be required to study this plan and then be quizzed on what he can remember about it." On the next page is a copy of the floor plan. Study it for five minutes, turn the page and see if you qualify for membership.

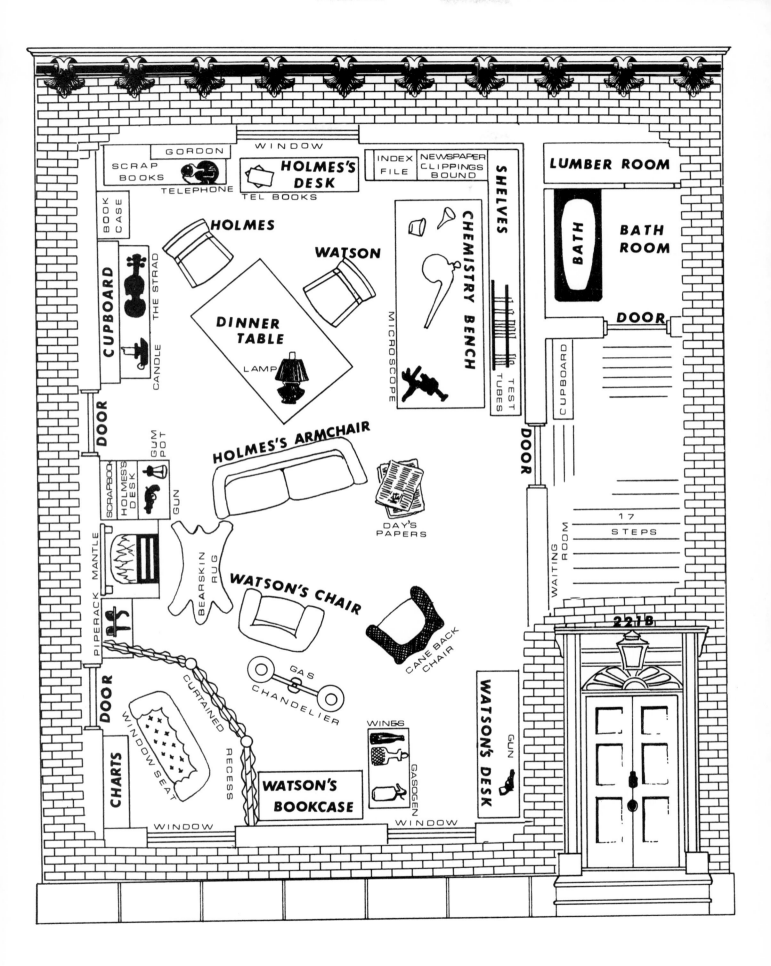

THE SHERLOCK HOLMES OBSERVATIONAL TEST

Use the diagram on the right to write in your answers. Check answers on Page 23.

(1) Where is Holmes's gun? Watson's gun?
(2) Where is the lumber room?
(3) Draw in Holmes's armchair.
(4) Where is the Stradivarius?
(5) Draw in the window seat.
(6) What is on the dinner table?
(7) Where is the microscope?
(8) Where is the telephone?
(9) Where is the index file?
(10) Where are the day's papers?
(11) Where is the gasogen?
(12) Where is the cupboard?
(13) How many steps are there up to Holmes's door?
(14) Where is the piperack?
(15) Where are the charts kept?
(16) Where is Watson's desk?
(17) Where is the gum pot?
(18) Draw in Watson's chair.
(19) Where are the scrapbooks? (two places)
(20) Where is the candle?
(21) Where is the bookcase?
(22) Where are the wine bottles?
(23) Draw in the gas chandelier.
(24) Where are the test tubes?
(25) What is on the floor in front of the fireplace?
(26) Where are the telephone books?
(27) Where is Watson's bookcase?
(28) Where is Holmes's dinner table chair?
(29) Draw in the caneback chair.
(30) Where are the bound newspaper clippings?
(31) Where is General Gordon's picture hung?
(32) Where is the chemistry bench?

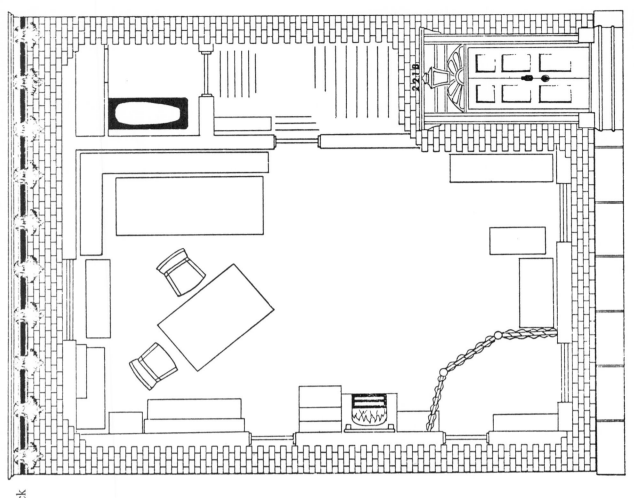

24

A Movie Detective Quiz

Detective story fans, gather near, for I have a challenging quiz for you. Below is a list of twenty-six fictional detectives and villains that have appeared in the movies over the last forty years. Next to this list is another list of the actors who portrayed them on the screen. Your job is to match up detective (or villain) and actor. Twenty right would be a good score.

Detectives and Villains	Movie Actors
(A) Lew Archer	(1) William Powell
(B) Charlie Chan	(2) Tom Conway
(C) James Bond	(3) Ralph Bellamy
(D) Boston Blackie	(4) Robert Montgomery
(E) Father Brown	(5) Basil Rathbone
(F) Nick Charles (The Thin Man)	(6) Humphrey Bogart
(G) Simon Templar (The Saint)	(7) Paul Newman
(H) Harry Palmer	(8) Sean Connery
(I) The Falcon	(9) Henry Daniell
(J) Dr. Fu Manchu	(10) Tony Randall
(K) Matt Helm	(11) Lloyd Nolan
(L) Sherlock Holmes	(12) Jack Hawkins
(M) Professor Moriarty	(13) Chester Morris
(N) Inspector Maigret	(14) Warner Baxter
(O) Philip Marlow	(15) Sidney Poitier
(P) Mr. Moto	(16) Edward Arnold
(Q) Hercule Poirot	(17) Boris Karloff
(R) Ellery Queen	(18) Ian Carmichael
(S) Raffles	(19) Warner Oland
(T) Michael Shayne	(20) Alec Guinness
(U) Sam Spade	(21) Michael Caine
(V) Virgil Tibbs	(22) David Niven
(W) Lord Peter Wimsey	(23) Jean Gabin
(X) Nero Wolfe	(24) Peter Lorre
(Y) The Crime Doctor	(25) Warner Baxter
(Z) Gideon of Scotland Yard	(26) George Sanders

BATTER UP!

atter up! The cry of summer is heard across the land and joy enters the heart. Baseball, for those that have played it or watched it, invariably brings to mind the joys of youth and the empty lots we first played the game on. But what of winter or rain? Must we forsake this pleasant pastime? Never! All we need are a pair of dice and the following instructions and we can play baseball all year-round. First, draw a baseball diamond to keep track of the runners on base. Checkers will serve very well for base runners. It is best to play the game with two players, although it can also be played as a solitaire game. Make up a scorecard (see below). The play is the same as in regular baseball with ties settled by going into extra innings. Each player, in turn, rolls the dice for his half-inning until he has made three outs and then he enters his score. The play value of each roll of the dice is as follows:

2 (1+1)   =   This is a homerun.
3 (1+2)   =   This is a strikeout.
4 (3+1)   =   This is a strikeout.
4 (2+2)   =   This is a base on balls.
5   =   The batter grounds out. If there are any runners on base, then the batter is out and the lead runner is also out.
6 (4+2, 5+1) =   Batter grounds out, all runners advance one base.
6 (3+3)   =   Fielding error, batter safe, all runners advance one base.
7   =   Batter flies out, all runners hold base.
8 (6+2, 5+3) =   Batter flies out. Runners on second and third advance one base, runner on first stays put.
8 (4+4)   =   This is a base on balls.

9   =   This is a single, all runners advance one base.
10   =   Double, all runners advance two bases.
11   =   Triple, all runners score.
12   =   Homerun, everybody scores.

If you have men on base and wish to sacrifice, the play values are as follows:

2 or 12   =   Batter and lead runner are out.
3 or 11   =   Batter safe, all runners advance.
5, 7 or 9   =   Batter is out, no advance.
4, 6, 8 or 10   =   Batter out, all runners advance.

	1	2	3	4	5	6	7	8	9
Player 1									
Player 2									

veryone on Merlin's Isle is nervously looking over his shoulders these days. It is rumored that the dreaded Chicken-man has come down out of the mountains from the Forest of No Return. Industrial pollution is said to be the cause of breaking the spell which had kept him locked within the Tree of 10,000 Thorns. It seems that the thorns all fell off the tree, setting this fearsome ogre free after 700 years of prickly imprisonment. To say that he is a bit irritable would be putting it mildly.

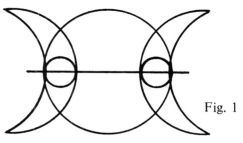

Fig. 1

So, if you chance to meet up with him you had better take up a stick and make the sign of the Double-Horned Zat on the ground and stand in the middle of it until he flies away. (see Fig. 1). When drawing the sign you must do it with one continuous line. Also, no part of the line may cross over any other part of the line.

Now, practice well, you never know when you may hear the flap, flap, flap of giant chicken wings.

surveyor stopped by the Grits-N-Bits coffee shop the other day and told about a job he had just finished. Two farmers had bought five square acres of land that had divided their farms and had asked him to lay out a straight fence that would divide their purchase into two equal parcels of land. After much thought, the surveyor came up with the answer. The only trouble is that he left town before telling anyone how he did it. Can you tell the folks at the Grits-N-Bits how it was done?

GLEN RIDGE CALDWELL VERONA

C.B.T.

was going over my ninth-grade yearbook from Glen Ridge High the other day when I came across this drawing I made depicting a scene in our cafeteria. I worked in the cafeteria during lunchtime, and when some of the characters brought their trays back they looked like jugglers in the Barnum and Bailey circus. Merlin suggested that I use the picture as a theme for some dinner table puzzles, so students, pull your chairs up to the table and pay attention.

DEFYING GRAVITY

You will need a small milk bottle (or an empty glass jar) and a marble for this brain buster. Place the marble in the bottle and challenge someone to pick the bottle up, walk across the room and place it on another table. The catch is that they have to pick the bottle up by the bottom and turn it upside down before starting across the room. The marble must not fall out and they cannot of course place anything over the top of the bottle.

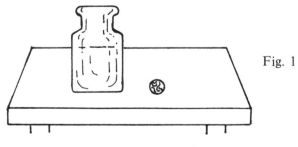

Fig. 1

SUGAR-JUGGLING

This is a sweet little trick to fool your friends with. Hold a small paper cup in your hand as shown in Fig. 2. Next, place two lumps of sugar, one on top of the other, between your thumb and first finger.

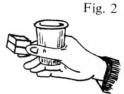
Fig. 2

Your problem is to toss the lumps of sugar, one by one, into the air and catch them in the cup. The first lump is easy, but when you try to catch the second lump the first usually flies out of the cup. The secret to catching the second lump while keeping the first one in the cup is to release the second lump, not throw it in the air, and quickly drop the cup under it. With a little practice you should be able to master this bit of juggling and perplex your friend with your dexterity.

THE FAMOUS PAPER BRIDGE

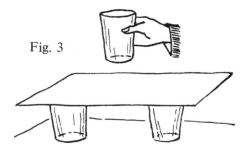
Fig. 3

Now, here is a good way to win an egg salad sandwich the next time you find yourself in a cafeteria with some friends. Put two glasses on the table a short distance apart and place a sheet of fairly stiff paper across the tops of the glasses. Next, state that you have the power to hypnotize the paper and make it strong enough to support a third glass placed in the middle of the paper (see Fig. 3). This puzzle is a good stumper, so give it a try before looking in the back of the book for the solution.

A LOOPY PROBLEM

You should have a lot of fun with this puzzle. Form a one-inch wide loop of stiff paper (Fig. 4). Place this loop on top of an empty milk bottle (or glass jar). On top of the loop, directly over the mouth of the bottle, place a dime. Your problem is to get the dime into the bottle. When doing this you are only allowed to touch the paper loop. You are also only allowed to use one hand while solving this puzzle. Good luck, students!

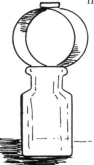
Fig. 4

CHUG-A-MUG

Fig. 5

Our last academic problem is a tough one. Take a long piece of string and tie it to the handle of a soup mug. Next, tie the other end to some overhead support. The mug should be about two feet above the ground. Now, your problem is to take a pair of scissors and cut the string in half at a point about two feet above the mug in such a manner that the mug will not fall to the floor. Only the scissors may touch the string. Nothing can be touching the mug and you cannot have anything between the floor and the mug. This is strictly a pass-fail test.

The Haunted House

The old MacAllister mansion outside of Lloydville has stood empty and forlorn now for many years owing to its ghostly inhabitants. To shed some light on the subject a committee of experts from P.O.P. (Pals of Poltergeists) spent a night there one summer. They met five ghosts who locked them in the main hall and would not set them free until they had correctly answered a problem put to them by each of the apparitions. Let's see how long you would have been held a prisoner in the MacAllister house. (See page 31 for picture of main hall.)

(1) The first ghost pointed to the plaque on the wall above the fireplace and said, "On that plaque is the MacAllister family motto. Ten of the letters have fallen off. Tell me what the original motto said."

S_R_K_ W_I_E _H_
I_O_'S H_T

(2) The second ghost pointed a finger at a spider's web high above our heads and asked, "If the arc of that web describes a quarter of a circle and is 20 inches long, what is the area covered by the web in square inches?"

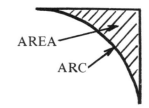

AREA—
ARC—

(3) The third specter pointed to the sections of chain which lay upon the floor and said, "Last night I found these nine sections of chain down in the dungeon. The original chain was composed of fifty links. If it costs 25¢ to open a link and 50¢ to close and weld it, what is the least amount of money it will cost me to have it put back together again?"

(4) The fourth shade placed a small checkerboard on the table and positioned nine checkers on the numbered squares. "You must remove eight of the checkers from the board leaving the ninth one in the center square. You remove a checker by jumping another one over it to the vacant square beyond. You can jump in any direction using any checker. Any number of jumps in succession with the same checker will count as one move. Your problem is to do it in the least number of moves."

(5) With an eerie laugh, the last ghost pointed around the room at the three clocks and whispered, "Yesterday, June 15, 1974, at 12:00 noon these three clocks were set going at precisely the same time. Twenty-four hours later the first clock was found to be one minute slow, the second clock one minute fast, and the third exactly on time. If the clocks are allowed to keep running on, losing or gaining a minute each day, on what date and what time of day will all three clocks show twelve o'clock again at the same instant?"

SRK WIE H
IO'SHT

31

our car is ready, so please hurry along, we don't want to be late. Merlin is giving a party tonight and he has hired England's home of mystery, Maskelyne's famous Egyptian Hall in Piccadilly, for the evening's entertainment. Merlin informs me that he has summoned many of the outstanding magicians and practitioners of mystery to perform tonight.

The theme of the evening is "Mysteries of The Early Conjurors." We should be seeing such personages as Houdini, Professor Hoffmann, DeKolta, Will Goldston, Kellar, Charles Bertram, Professor Pepper, etc. Also, puzzles will no doubt be presented by Maskelyne and Cooke's two automatons, Psycho and Zoe. Professor Stodare is also on hand and he will once again be exhibiting his illusion, The Sphinx.

There's the theater up ahead. Driver, please pull over and let us out here. By the look of things I believe we arrived just in time.

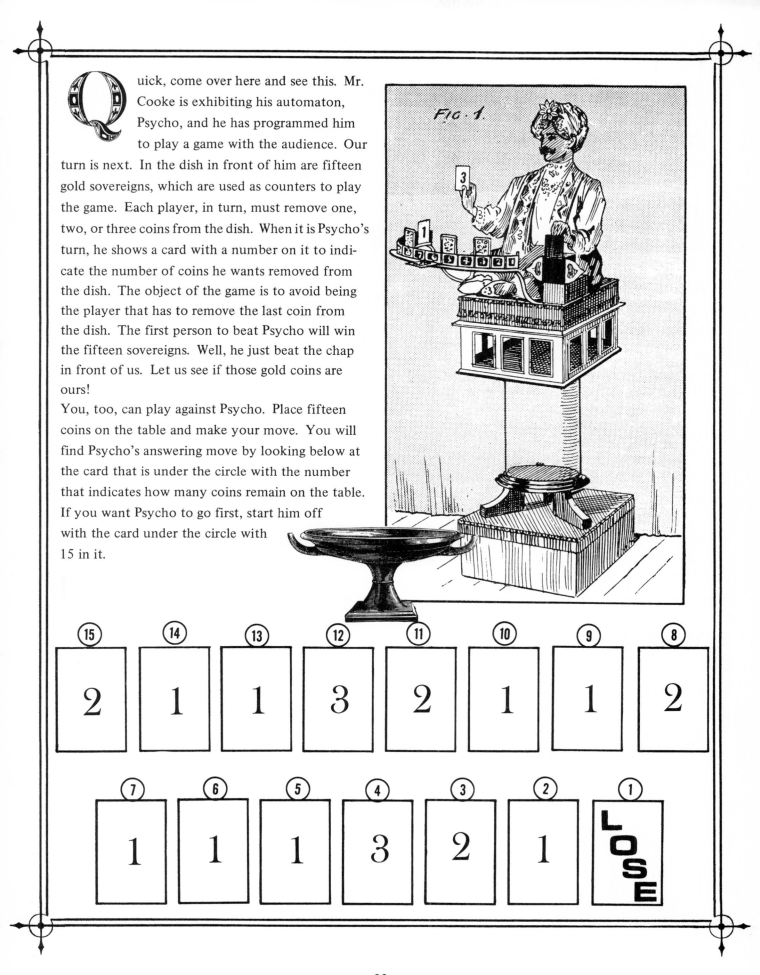

Quick, come over here and see this. Mr. Cooke is exhibiting his automaton, Psycho, and he has programmed him to play a game with the audience. Our turn is next. In the dish in front of him are fifteen gold sovereigns, which are used as counters to play the game. Each player, in turn, must remove one, two, or three coins from the dish. When it is Psycho's turn, he shows a card with a number on it to indicate the number of coins he wants removed from the dish. The object of the game is to avoid being the player that has to remove the last coin from the dish. The first person to beat Psycho will win the fifteen sovereigns. Well, he just beat the chap in front of us. Let us see if those gold coins are ours!

You, too, can play against Psycho. Place fifteen coins on the table and make your move. You will find Psycho's answering move by looking below at the card that is under the circle with the number that indicates how many coins remain on the table. If you want Psycho to go first, start him off with the card under the circle with 15 in it.

FIG. 1.

(15)	(14)	(13)	(12)	(11)	(10)	(9)	(8)
2	1	1	3	2	1	1	2

(7)	(6)	(5)	(4)	(3)	(2)	(1)
1	1	1	3	2	1	LOSE

ook at this now, Maskelyne and Cooke's "Wonder Of The Age," an electronic computer that solves forever that mathematical mystery, the Magic Square. It goes on to say that the "MAC" computer, which is locked in the basement vault of the Egyptian Hall, is connected by wires to the typewriter on this table. This is all very hard to believe, you know, even if it is 1890. Let's see now; it says that Mr. Cooke, who is at the table, can communicate with MAC by using that telegraph key in front of him. He will relay any number that you give him, say between 40 and 100, and the computer will immediately calculate the square and print it out on the Columbia Typewriter for you. This I have got to see! "Mr. Cooke, I challenge that infernal machine of yours to construct a square using my age, 47, as the magic number."

"I assure you, sir, that if your age were 147 or a biblical 1047, MAC would not fail. Stand back and witness the wonder of this or any other age, big MAC."

Well, bless my soul, look at that. The typewriter has come alive, and look, it is printing a Magic Square. Why, I don't believe my eyes, it seems to total 47 in every direction. Now how did they do it, man, how did they do it?

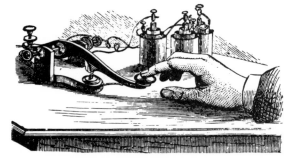

THE SECRET MATHEMATICAL FORMULA

GIVEN NUMBER **47**
ALWAYS SUBTRACT **30**
DIVIDE BY **4 (17(4** DIVIDEND
16
1 REMAINDER

A	B	C	D
⑦	⑩	⑬ +	
E ⑫ +	**F** ①	**G** ⑥	**H** ⑪
I ②	**J** ⑮ +	**K** ⑧	**L** ⑤
M ⑨	**N** ④	**O** ③	**P** ⑭ +

Fig. 1

Mr. Cooke has graciously consented to let the readers of *Merlin's* in on the secret of creating a Magic Square. At the bottom of page 34 you will find the secret mathematical formula needed to work this puzzle out. Follow closely: Take the number 47 (remember that you can do this with any number greater than 40); subtract 30 from it; divide the difference (17) by 4. This will leave you with a dividend of 4 and a remainder of 1. Next, look at Fig. 1 on page 34. In each one of the squares you will find a number in a circle (except for square D). This is the initial value of the square. You must add the dividend (4) to this value to get the final value for the square. For square D you must enter only the value of the dividend, (4). In the four squares that have a plus sign (+) next to the circled initial amount (squares, C, E, J, P), you must also add the remainder (1) from your calculation to get the final value for the square. Our sample square would be: (A) 7+4=11, (B) 10+4=14, (C) 13+4+1=18, (D) 0+4=4, (E) 12+4+1 = 17, (F) 1+4=5, (G) 6+4=10, (H) 11+4=15, (I) 2+4=6, (J) 15+4+1=20, (K) 8+4=12, (L) 5+4=9, (M) 9+4=13, (N) 4+4=8, (O) 3+4=7, (P) 14+4+1=19.

You can make up squares for very large numbers, say the year you were born. With a little practice, and some memorizing, you can actually learn to do this in your head. Why, you might even bill yourself as "The Eighth Wonder of the World, the Walking Computer."

THIS HISTORICAL MATHEMATICAL PUZZLE IS KNOWN AS A MAGIC SQUARE

THIS MAGIC SQUARE HAS BEEN ELECTRONICALLY COMPUTED BY THE MAC COMPUTER TO TOTAL 47 WHEN ADDED IN ANY DIRECTION. THE COMBINATIONS ARE:

A, B, C, D	E, F, G, H
I, J, K, L	M, N, O, P
A, F, K, P	M, J, G, D
A, D, M, P	F, G, J, K
I, J, M, N	A, B, E, F
C, D, G, H	K, L, O, P
E, I, H, L	B, C, N, O
A, E, I, M	B, F, J, N
C, G, K, O	D, H, L, P

A	B	C	D
11	**14**	**18**	**4**
E	F	G	H
17	**5**	**10**	**15**
I	J	K	L
6	**20**	**12**	**9**
M	N	O	P
13	**8**	**7**	**19**

PROGRAM PROBLEMS

ere are our seats. Let us settle down and peruse the program before the curtain goes up. Look at this, they have a puzzle section in the program. I think I'll try a few, since we have several minutes to go before show time.

Now, the first puzzle is an interesting one. It seems that a farmer owned twenty-one cows. He was very protective towards them and wished to enclose them in four fenced-in pastures. For some unknown reason he stipulated to the fence builder that each enclosure must hold an odd number of cows. Now, how in the world was he to do that?

Problem number 2 is one of those delightful area divisional problems. It stipulates that the square in the picture must be divided into six perfect squares. This is to be accomplished by drawing four straight lines across the square. An interesting puzzle!

Ah ha, here is an old favorite of mine. In puzzle number 3 you must place the four white counters and the four black counters in the sixteen squares of the diagram in such a way that no two counters of the same color will be in the same row, horizontally, vertically, or diagonally. Try this one, it's not as easy as it looks.

Here is a problem from Merlin. He states that to test the quickness of mind of three candidates for knighthood he had them solve the following problem. First, he showed them five helmets. Three of the helmets were white and the other two were gray. Next, he instructed them to close their eyes. Once they had done this, he placed a gray helmet on one man and a white helmet on each of the other two men. He then told them to open their eyes, look at each other, and then state what color helmet they were wearing and how they knew the color. You have just enough time to solve this one before the curtain goes up.

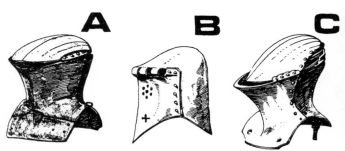

Charles Bertram

The first act is Charles Bertram, the famous Edwardian magician. Known as "The Royal Conjurer," he has appeared many times at the Egyptian Hall. A great manipulative artist, he will show many of his famous card tricks tonight. He has contributed to this book an interesting rope trick called Here, There, Everywhere. The magician picks up a piece of rope and shows it to the audience. There are three knots tied in the rope. On one of the end knots there hangs a solid metal ring (Fig. 3). He passes the rope behind his back and the ring jumps to the knot at the other end of the rope (Fig. 4). He once again passes the rope behind his back and the ring jumps back to the other end (Fig. 3). The third time he does this, the ring is found to have jumped to the middle knot (Fig. 5). The magician immediately hands the rope, with the ring still tied to the middle knot, out for inspection.

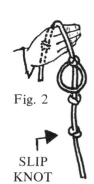

Fig. 1

The secret lies in the fact that there is a fourth knot tied in the rope. This knot is hidden by the performer's hand, which covers the knot when he holds the rope (Fig. 2). Also, the bottom knot on the rope is a slip knot (Fig. 1 and Fig. 2).

To perform: The performer picks up the rope with his right hand concealing the extra knot (Fig. 2) and holds it up to the audience (Fig. 3). When he passes the rope behind his back, the left hand takes the end with the extra knot and covers it. The rope is brought out and shown (Fig. 4). The previous action is reversed for the next pass. During the final pass behind your back, you pull the rope tight so that the slip knot will come apart and disappear. When you bring the rope out now, you do not cover the extra knot. The ring will be on the middle knot. Another miracle!

Fig. 2

SLIP
KNOT

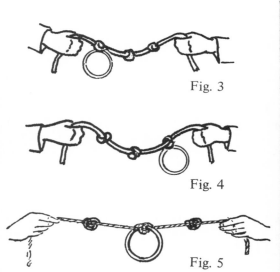

Fig. 3

Fig. 4

Fig. 5

THE STAGE AT THE EGYPTIAN HALL

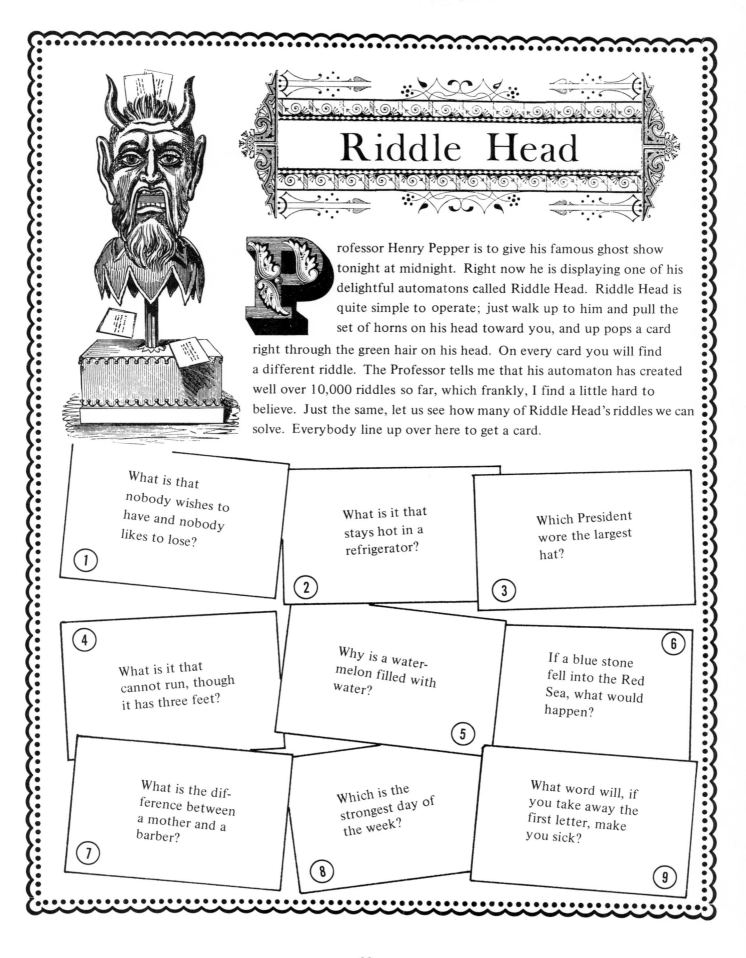

Riddle Head

Professor Henry Pepper is to give his famous ghost show tonight at midnight. Right now he is displaying one of his delightful automatons called Riddle Head. Riddle Head is quite simple to operate; just walk up to him and pull the set of horns on his head toward you, and up pops a card right through the green hair on his head. On every card you will find a different riddle. The Professor tells me that his automaton has created well over 10,000 riddles so far, which frankly, I find a little hard to believe. Just the same, let us see how many of Riddle Head's riddles we can solve. Everybody line up over here to get a card.

1. What is that nobody wishes to have and nobody likes to lose?

2. What is it that stays hot in a refrigerator?

3. Which President wore the largest hat?

4. What is it that cannot run, though it has three feet?

5. Why is a watermelon filled with water?

6. If a blue stone fell into the Red Sea, what would happen?

7. What is the difference between a mother and a barber?

8. Which is the strongest day of the week?

9. What word will, if you take away the first letter, make you sick?

TRANSPOSITION

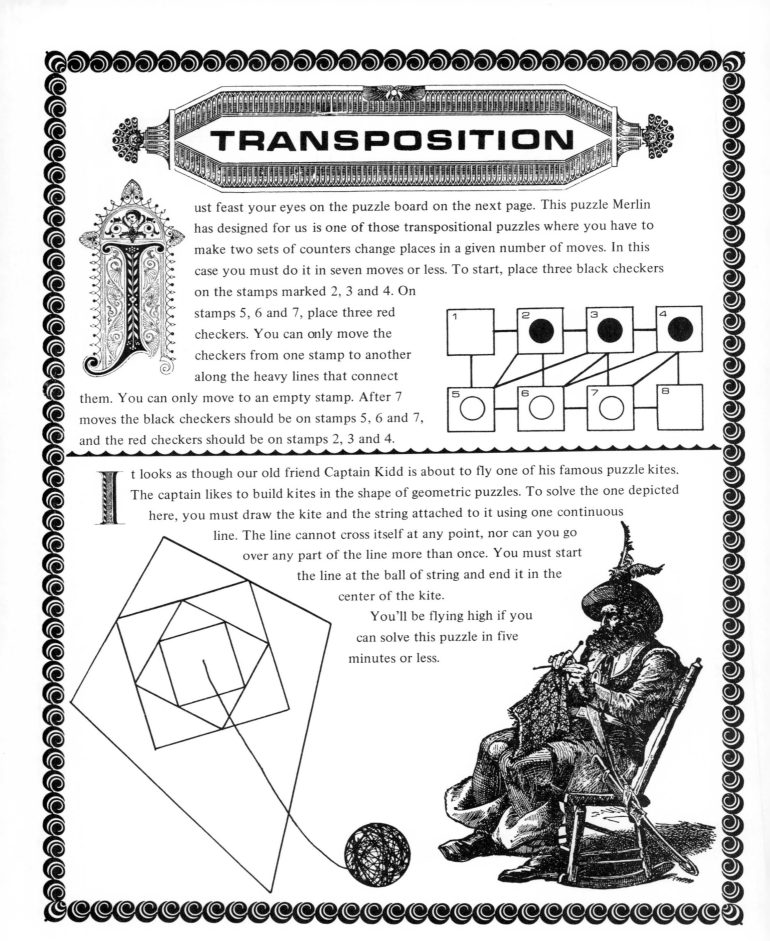

ust feast your eyes on the puzzle board on the next page. This puzzle Merlin has designed for us is one of those transpositional puzzles where you have to make two sets of counters change places in a given number of moves. In this case you must do it in seven moves or less. To start, place three black checkers on the stamps marked 2, 3 and 4. On stamps 5, 6 and 7, place three red checkers. You can only move the checkers from one stamp to another along the heavy lines that connect them. You can only move to an empty stamp. After 7 moves the black checkers should be on stamps 5, 6 and 7, and the red checkers should be on stamps 2, 3 and 4.

t looks as though our old friend Captain Kidd is about to fly one of his famous puzzle kites. The captain likes to build kites in the shape of geometric puzzles. To solve the one depicted here, you must draw the kite and the string attached to it using one continuous line. The line cannot cross itself at any point, nor can you go over any part of the line more than once. You must start the line at the ball of string and end it in the center of the kite.

You'll be flying high if you can solve this puzzle in five minutes or less.

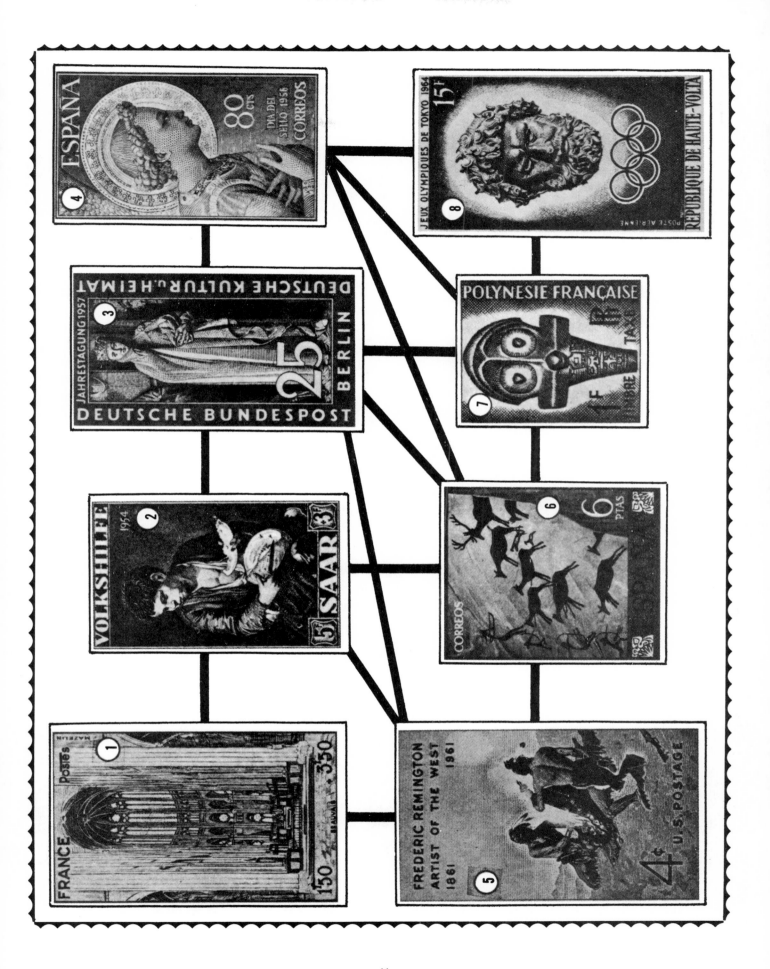

PuzzleRock

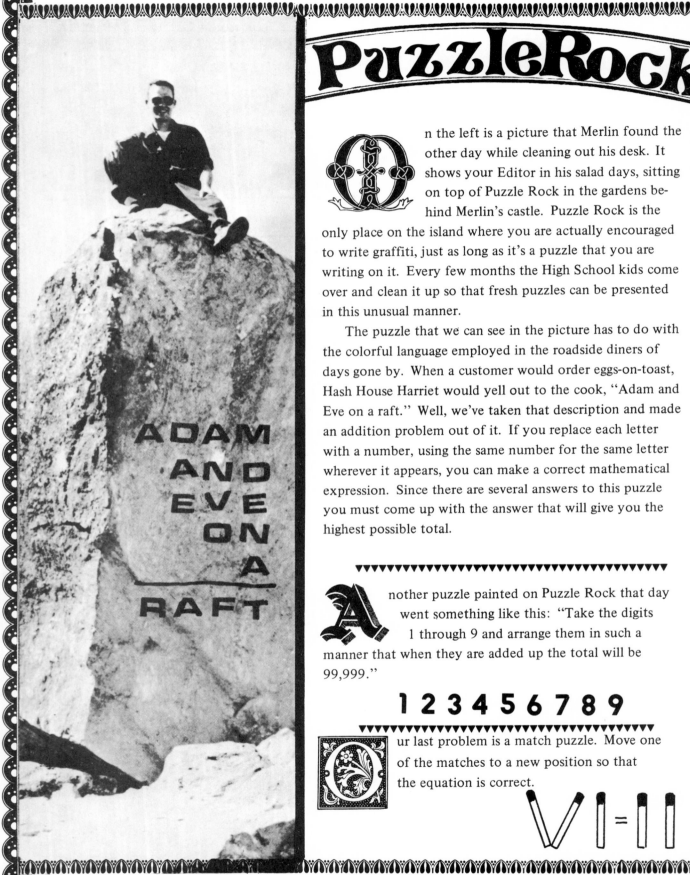

ADAM
AND
EVE
ON
A
RAFT

On the left is a picture that Merlin found the other day while cleaning out his desk. It shows your Editor in his salad days, sitting on top of Puzzle Rock in the gardens behind Merlin's castle. Puzzle Rock is the only place on the island where you are actually encouraged to write graffiti, just as long as it's a puzzle that you are writing on it. Every few months the High School kids come over and clean it up so that fresh puzzles can be presented in this unusual manner.

The puzzle that we can see in the picture has to do with the colorful language employed in the roadside diners of days gone by. When a customer would order eggs-on-toast, Hash House Harriet would yell out to the cook, "Adam and Eve on a raft." Well, we've taken that description and made an addition problem out of it. If you replace each letter with a number, using the same number for the same letter wherever it appears, you can make a correct mathematical expression. Since there are several answers to this puzzle you must come up with the answer that will give you the highest possible total.

Another puzzle painted on Puzzle Rock that day went something like this: "Take the digits 1 through 9 and arrange them in such a manner that when they are added up the total will be 99,999."

1 2 3 4 5 6 7 8 9

Our last problem is a match puzzle. Move one of the matches to a new position so that the equation is correct.

WILL GOLDSTON Ltd.

ALADDIN HOUSE, 14 GREEN STREET,
LEICESTER SQUARE, LONDON, W.C.2

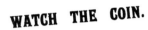

No. 126. The Latest Egg Vanish.

178. The "Last Word" Rising Card Trick.

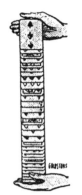

No. 164. The Pack of Cards of Enchantment.

354. Goldston's Sliding Die Box Trick.

WATCH THE COIN.

An ordinary tumbler is placed on the table upside down over a borrowed coin. A cover to fit over the glass is made out of a sheet of newspaper. The tumbler is lifted together with the paper cover — the company are requested to note that the coin is head upward. Again the coin is covered, and the conjuror brings down his hand on the tumbler with a thud; to the surprise of the company, instead of the tumbler being smashed, the paper crumples, the tumbler having vanished.

EXPLANATION: When the performer lifts the tumbler covered with the paper, he silently allows the glass to fall out on to his lap as he calls attention to the coin. To make the trick effective, the conjuror should bring his hand down on the paper cover with some force.

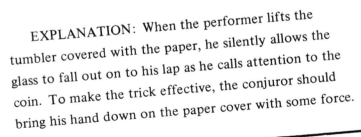

A trick from Will Goldston's "Catalogue of Magic", circa 1930.

The Famous Linking Rings.

No. 166G.
The Mysterious Reels of Cotton.

No. 332. The Chair or Table Lifting.

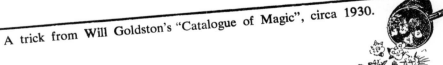

No. 351. The Plush Changing Bag.

43

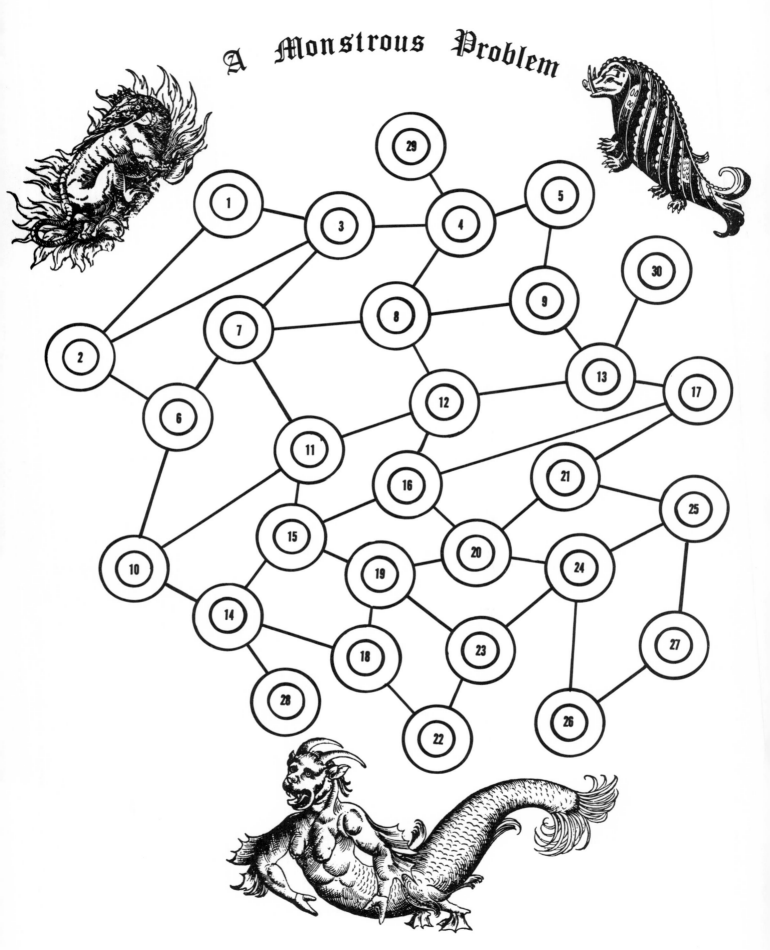

A Monstrous Problem

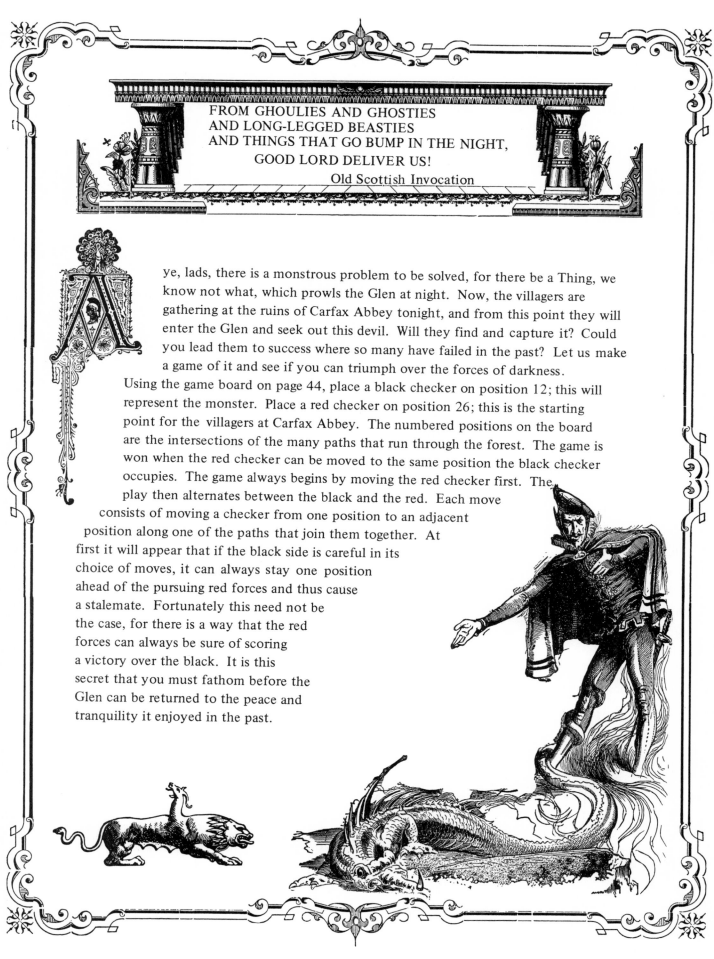

ye, lads, there is a monstrous problem to be solved, for there be a Thing, we know not what, which prowls the Glen at night. Now, the villagers are gathering at the ruins of Carfax Abbey tonight, and from this point they will enter the Glen and seek out this devil. Will they find and capture it? Could you lead them to success where so many have failed in the past? Let us make a game of it and see if you can triumph over the forces of darkness.

Using the game board on page 44, place a black checker on position 12; this will represent the monster. Place a red checker on position 26; this is the starting point for the villagers at Carfax Abbey. The numbered positions on the board are the intersections of the many paths that run through the forest. The game is won when the red checker can be moved to the same position the black checker occupies. The game always begins by moving the red checker first. The play then alternates between the black and the red. Each move consists of moving a checker from one position to an adjacent position along one of the paths that join them together. At first it will appear that if the black side is careful in its choice of moves, it can always stay one position ahead of the pursuing red forces and thus cause a stalemate. Fortunately this need not be the case, for there is a way that the red forces can always be sure of scoring a victory over the black. It is this secret that you must fathom before the Glen can be returned to the peace and tranquility it enjoyed in the past.

Well, here we are at last, inside Merlin's Crystal Palace looking down the south transept. There must be a thousand exhibits under this glass

roof to choose from. Let's try this one over here. This exhibit is sponsored by a paper manufacturer. I suppose they are here because there are so many good puzzles and tricks that employ paper in their performance. The company's representative, Pierre DeForester, is presenting some paper problems now. Let's listen!

HEAVEN AND HELL

"I once heard a story concerning Greed that I would like to pass on to you. It seems that two souls confronted St. Peter at the gates of Heaven and asked to come in. St. Peter told them that there was but room for one of them and that they must therefore draw lots to see who was the worthier. St. Peter then took a sheet of paper and folded it once, then once again, and finally a third time. (See Figures 1, 2, 3, and 4.) He then tore the folded sheet of paper into two unequal portions (Fig. 5) and was about to speak when one of the two souls knocked the other aside and reached out and grabbed the larger portion of paper. 'I have the bigger piece,' he shouted. 'I won, let me in!' 'Quiet,' commanded St. Peter, 'let us see what these lots tell us. The smaller piece belongs to this gentleman who has yet to speak. If we open it up we find that it is in the shape of a cross (Fig. 6). Now, let me have the piece that you took from me. Before we open it up we will tear it down the middle (Fig. 7). Now, open up the pieces and see what they have to tell you.' When he did so the poor man found that the pieces formed the word <u>HELL</u> (Fig. 8). Seeing his fate clearly written before him the man turned to go, but St. Peter bade him enter along with the other man saying, 'There is always room for one more up here and I can see from this lesson that greed has been driven out of your heart for good.' I'd say that's a pretty good lesson for all of us."

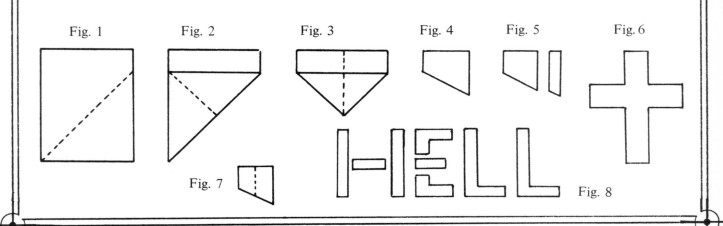

Fig. 1   Fig. 2   Fig. 3   Fig. 4   Fig. 5   Fig. 6

Fig. 7   Fig. 8

TINTINNABULATION

Ladies and Gentlemen, this is certainly one of the finest tintinnabulous puzzles that I have ever seen. Step a little closer, please, so that you can examine the paper puzzle that I am holding in my hand. (See Fig. 1.) It is constructed of three fairly stiff pieces of paper. The puzzle, Ladies and Gentlemen, is to discover just how they were put together without tearing or mutilating any of the fragile pieces. Please note that the paper bell is firmly locked onto the large paper link by the smaller paper link. The hole in the small link, however, is far too small for either side of the bell to pass through it. How was it done? A ringing solution from one of you is needed. Now! Who would like to try it first? (Note: The three pieces to the puzzle are shown in Figures 2, 3, and 4. They are drawn in the correct proportions for the working of this puzzle.)

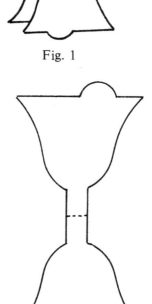

Fig. 1

Fig. 2

Fig. 3

BELLZEBUB

Your friends will think that this is a Devil of a trick if you do it well. Pass a length of rope and a stiff piece of paper in the shape of a bell to your audience for examination. Next, have someone thread the bell onto the rope and then have him tie each end of the rope to your wrists. (See Fig. 5.) You can even have him seal the knots with tape. Lastly, have him drape a large cloth over your arms so that your hands, the rope and the bell are out of sight. In ten seconds flat you drop the cloth and show that the paper bell has been removed undamaged from the rope and that your hands are still securely tied. The rope and bell may once more be examined. How are you to do this masterful magical feat of matter through matter? You must have *two* identical paper bells. (How else?) The second paper bell is in the inside pocket of your jacket. Raise your arms chest high. Under cover of the cloth, tear the bell off of the rope, crumple it up, and slip it into your inside jacket pocket. Remove the other paper bell and the trick is done. You might also try secreting the second bell up the sleeve of your jacket instead of in your coat.

Fig. 4

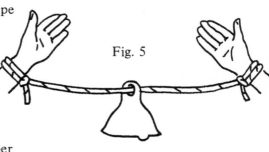

Fig. 5

"Mr. DeForester, these feats are amazing! Please show us some more!"

47

The Idle Hours Country Club

t the Idle Hours Country Club the players are out early this morning. Come over here on the veranda for a moment, I want to show you something. Over there is our tennis area. There seems to be a lively game in progress. You'll notice that the chalk lines outlining the court are getting rather thin. As soon as the game is over Mr. Rakencut, our grounds keeper, will rechalk them with a new machine the club has bought from Professor Pepper called the Steam Man. All you have to do is to fire up his boiler and program him to do any job around the club. The Steam Man uses one of the roller-type markers. Once he puts it down he can't pick it up again without making a mess of the job. We have worked out a route for him to take so that he can mark off the court using one continuous line. It is impossible, of course, to do this without going over some of the lines twice. The route we worked out is the shortest possible one, one that goes over the least number of lines twice. Here is a sketch of the court with the lengths of the lines in feet (Fig. 1). See if you can discover the route that the Steam Man will take.

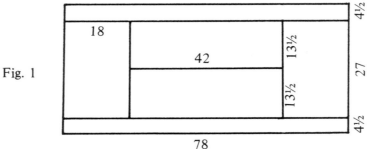

Fig. 1

18   42   13½   4½

13½   27

4½   78

48

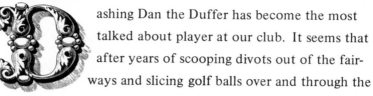ashing Dan the Duffer has become the most talked about player at our club. It seems that after years of scooping divots out of the fairways and slicing golf balls over and through the club house, Dan has finally gotten his game together. The strange thing about it is that no matter what wood or iron he hits the golf ball with, it travels only one of two distances. Dan has worked it out so that by combining these two shots, sometimes hitting two long shots and one short shot as an example, he can play the front nine of our course in twenty-six strokes.

Now Dan always plays in a straight line from tee to cup, his hooks and slices being a thing of the past. Also, he sometimes will hit the ball past the green and have to hit back to the green to hole out. It makes no difference to him, he is always able to sink the ball by hitting it one of two distances. Our problem is to try and calculate what the two distances are that Dan uses in hitting his way to fame and fortune. The yardage for the first nine holes on our course is 150 yards, 300 yards, 250 yards, 325 yards, 275 yards, 350 yards, 225 yards, 400 yards, and 425 yards.

If you want to beat Dan at his own game, then you had better hurry up with the answer. Our group is on the tee next.

ver here is our Archery range. Those two lovely ladies warming up for the competition are the Hood sisters. They usually compete as a team. They are extremely good; so good in fact that no one knows which one is the better archer. Why, just last week in competition they scored exactly the same. They both put each of their three arrows in the same circles of the target and came up with a combined score of 96 points. If you were not there it makes a nice little puzzle to try and figure out which of the circles the arrows ended up in. Would you care to give it a try?

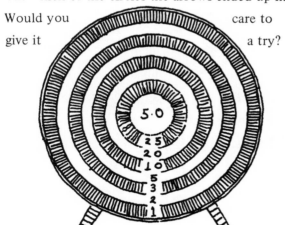

Bet-A-Million Wellington

et-A-Million Wellington, otherwise known as J. Wellington Moneybags, is back again to take on the suckers, er, I mean the sporting gentry among the visitors to Merlin's Isle. Wellington is a great gambler, and judging by the size of the diamond stickpin in his shirt front, a very successful one. So remember, forewarned is forearmed!

"All right, Ladies and Gentlemen, step right over here! Today may be your lucky day! I have here a simple little game that you may care to play with me. On this table I have placed twenty-four cards in four rows of six cards each (see drawing on next page). No card used is greater than a 6. The object of the game is either to score 31 points before your opponent, or cause your opponent to make a score greater than 31. Play alternates between the two contestants. The player who goes first may turn any card face down. Let's say he turns a 6 face down, he would then count 'six' aloud. The second player might then turn over a 3; adding the value to the 6, he would count aloud 'nine.' The first player would then go again, perhaps turning over a 5, adding this value to the 9 and declaring aloud 'four-teen.' Both players continue in this fashion until, as I said before, one declares 31 or the other is forced to turn over a card that would drive the accumulating score over 31. Now I ask you, could anything be fairer? I'll even let you go first although the winner of the last game usually has that honor. Oh, by the way, how about a little side bet to make things interesting? Would ten dollars be too rich for your blood?"

Is he kidding — ten dollars? If you threw your money into the river the action would be faster and the results would be just the same. If you must play with Wellington, then here are some play-ing tips. On the way to 31 you must always score one of the follow-ing sums on each of your turns: 3, 10, 17, 24 or 31.

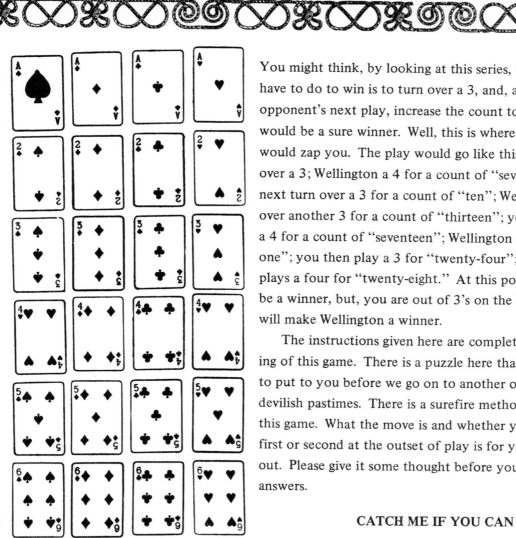

You might think, by looking at this series, that all you have to do to win is to turn over a 3, and, after your opponent's next play, increase the count to 10 and you would be a sure winner. Well, this is where Wellington would zap you. The play would go like this: you turn over a 3; Wellington a 4 for a count of "seven"; you next turn over a 3 for a count of "ten"; Wellington turns over another 3 for a count of "thirteen"; you turn over a 4 for a count of "seventeen"; Wellington a 4 for "twenty-one"; you then play a 3 for "twenty-four"; Wellington plays a four for "twenty-eight." At this point you should be a winner, but, you are out of 3's on the board, which will make Wellington a winner.

The instructions given here are complete for the playing of this game. There is a puzzle here that I am going to put to you before we go on to another of Wellington's devilish pastimes. There is a surefire method for winning this game. What the move is and whether you should go first or second at the outset of play is for you to reason out. Please give it some thought before you look at the answers.

CATCH ME IF YOU CAN

This is an aptly named betting puzzle. In the illustration we see Wellington holding the end of a bill with his right hand. His left hand is below, but not touching the bill. The thumb and index finger of his left hand are about one inch apart. In demonstrating this trick, Wellington drops the bill and catches it by closing the thumb and index fingers of his left hand before the bill falls to the ground. After doing this several times, Wellington will bet you that you cannot catch the bill in the same way. The catch is that Wellington will hold the bill while you place your left hand, just as he did with the fingers apart, halfway down the bill. Even if he offers you three to one odds don't bet with him. This is a most deceptive trick; it looks extremely easy, but it isn't. You may be lucky once or twice, but, you will soon find that it is almost impossible to catch a falling bill under these circumstances. Your reflexes are just not fast enough.

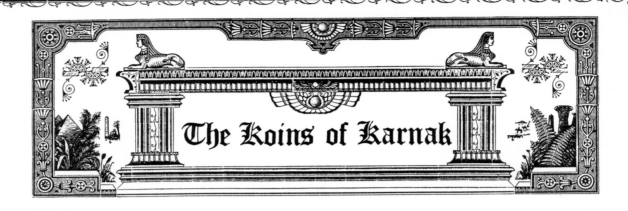

The Koins of Karnak

overs of games, step forward and harken to what I have to say. From a far-off land Merlin brings to us an ingenious game he calls "The Koins of Karnak." It is named after the vast temple complex that was at the center of that famous city of ancient Egypt, Thebes. Now Merlin claims that they played this game over 3,000 years ago. Since I wasn't there I'll not dispute his word. To set up the game, lay out twenty-five coins in five rows of five coins each. You can use the game board pictured in the Egyptian stele on page 53. Play alternates between players. In your turn you can remove any number of coins from any row or column. There cannot be, however, a gap between any of the coins removed. For example, if I remove the middle three coins in the top row my opponent cannot remove the two end coins on the left and right. He can, however, remove either one of them. Play continues until all the coins have been

removed. The loser is the player who is forced to remove the last coin. This is a very popular old game and Merlin feels that you should have many enjoyable hours attempting to master it. In my own research into its origins I find that the underlying theory as to skillful play has yet to be worked out by the mathematicians who have interested themselves in it.

One last thought before leaving you. Merlin feels that all of us should be more inventive in our approach to the fascinating diversions that are to be found within this book. When you have become proficient with this game, try it with six coins in six rows or four coins in eight rows. The possibilities are limitless.

Have fun.

Solutions

Page 1

The man with the black mask.

Page 2

(1)

(2)
Turn the 6 upside down. You now have a 9. The number we want is 931.

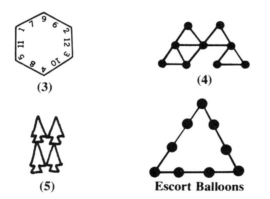

(3)

(4)

(5)

Escort Balloons

Page 4

(1) Drum Puzzle—The puzzle can be solved using 12 strokes. In the figure start at point <u>A</u> and follow the lines around to point <u>B</u>. The two curved lines are drawn one above the other.

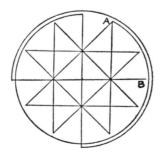

(2) The Garden Maze

(3) The First Prize Puzzle—Draw the figure on the donut. At one point the line you draw goes around the donut and comes up out of the hole, which happens to be in the center of one of the squares.

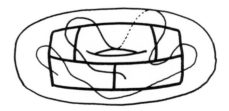

Page 6

(1) Start at any dot, count six dots and place a coin on the sixth dot. Remember which dot you *started* counting from as that's the dot you will want to place your second coin on. Start your second coin on a dot that will allow you to come to rest on the first dot. Start the third coin so that it comes to rest on the dot you started your second coin from. Continue like this for the rest of the coins. **(2)** Thirty-five triangles. **(3)** Move 2 and 3 to squares 9 and 10. Move 5 and 6 to squares 2 and 3. Move 8 and 9 to squares 5 and 6. Move 1 and 2 to squares 8 and 9.

Page 8

(1) P,   (2) G,   (3) Q,   (4) R,   (5) K,   (6) L,
(7) B,   (8) A,   (9) N,   (10) I,   (11) D,   (12) M.

Page 9

(1) 4 to 6   (2) 11 to 4   (3) 12 to 5   (4) 2 to 7   (5) 6 to 4
(6) 7 to 2   (7) 1 to 4   (8) 10 to 8   (9) 14 to 12   (10) 12 to 5
(11) 4 to 6   (12) 3 to 10   (13) 15 to 6.

Page 10

(1) It is time to get it fixed. (2) February, because it is the shortest month. (3) One ball, if it were long enough. (4) Samson. He brought down the house. (5) A donkey. (6) Your age. (7) A baseball team. (8) An elephant can have fleas but a flea cannot have elephants. (9) When it is made into little pats. (10) When it is ajar. (11) The library has the most stories. (12) Yesterday. (13) Your feet from off the floor. (14) When the cow jumped over the moon. (15) When he takes the floor. (16) Because it always advances with a bow. (17) Nothing. (18) The dictionary.

Page 11

The shortest route is of course a straight line. To visualize it you must unfold the walls of the room and lay them out flat. In figure A the route that appears to be the shortest is really the longest, being some 42 feet in length. Figure B comes close, but the distance is still slightly over 40 feet. Figure C has the correct solution, giving us a route of exactly 40 feet.

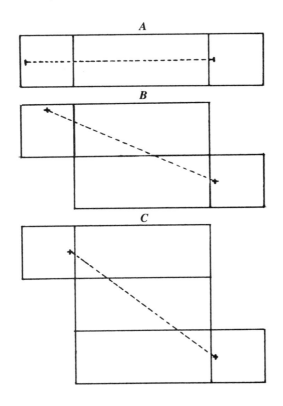

A

B

C

Page 12

The "English Sixteen" Puzzle—We know of no rule for working this puzzle. There are several possible solutions, including moving the men in the order listed below. The man to be moved is in each case indicated by the number of the square (page 13). As there is never more than one square vacant, it is not necessary to specify the square to which it is to be moved. We believe 52 to be the smallest number of moves that will suffice to transfer the whole of the men.

11, 7, 9, 8, 10, 13, 11, 14, 9, 6, 8, 5, 7, 11, 9, 10, 8, 2, 1, 6, 3, 5, 7,

4, 9, 12, 15, 17, 14, 16, 13, 15, 11, 7, 9, 14, 11, 13, 10, 8, 9, 6, 8, 2, 5, 7, 11, 9, 12, 10, 8, 9.

A Singular Subtraction—The number 45 is the sum of the digits 1, 2, 3, 4, 5, 6, 7, 8, 9. The puzzle is solved by arranging these in reverse order and subtracting the original series from them, the remainder consisting of the same digits in a different order and therefore making the same total—viz., 45.

$$987654321 = 45$$
$$123456789 = 45$$
$$864197532 = 45$$

A Mysterious Multiplicand—The number 37 answers the conditions of the problem. Multiplied by 3, it is 111; by 6, 222; by 9, 333; by 12, 444; by 15, 555; by 18, 666; by 21, 777; by 24, 888; and by 27, 999.

An Unmanageable Legacy—The lawyer had a horse of his own, which he drove into the stable with the rest. "Now," he said to John, "take your half." John took nine horses accordingly. James and William were then invited to take their shares, receiving six and two horses respectively. This division exactly disposed of the seventeen horses of the testator; and the lawyer, pocketing his fee, drove his own steed home again. This solution rests on the fact that the sum of the three fractions named, $\frac{1}{2}$, $\frac{1}{3}$, and $\frac{1}{9}$, when reduced to a common denominator, will be found not to amount to unity, but only to $\frac{17}{18}$. The addition of another horse ($=\frac{1}{18}$), bringing the total number up to eighteen, renders it divisible by such common denominator and enables each to get his proper share, the lawyer then resuming his own $\frac{1}{18}$, which he had lent for the purpose of the division. In the administration of the Mohammedan Law of Inheritance, which involves numerous and complicated fractions, this expedient is frequently employed.

A Novel Century—$9 \times 8 + 7 + 6 + 5 + 4 + 3 + 2 + 1 = 100$.

Page 14

The "Twenty-Six" Puzzle

		1	4	
	11	6	7	2
	8	10	3	5
		9	12	

Many Figures, But a Small Result—Reducing each fraction to its lowest denominator, it will be found to be equal to $\frac{1}{2}$, and $\frac{1}{2} + \frac{1}{2} = 1$.

$$\frac{35}{70} + \frac{148}{296}$$

The Captives in The Tower—The boy descended first, using the cannonball as a counterpoise. The queen and her daughter then took the cannonball out of the upper basket, and the daughter descended, the boy acting as counterpoise. The cannonball was then allowed to run down alone. When it reached the ground, the daughter got into the basket along with the cannonball, and their joint weight acted as counterpoise while the queen descended. The princess got out and the cannonball was sent down alone. The boy then went down, the cannonball ascending. The daughter removed the cannonball and went down alone, her brother ascending. The latter then put the cannonball in the opposite basket and lowered himself to the ground.

A Difficult Division—Each son's share will be seven casks (irrespective of contents), and of wine, 3½ casks. The division can be made in either of two ways: Dick and Tom each take 2 full, 2 empty, and 3 half-full casks and Harry, 3 full, 3 empty, and 1 half-full; or Dick and Tom take 3 full, 3 empty, and 1 half-full cask and Harry 1 full, 1 empty, and 5 half-full casks.

Nothing Left—The required number is 118. To obtain it, work the process indicated in reverse order, as follows:

$$0 + 18 = 18$$
$$18 \times 18 = 324$$
$$324 \div 3 = 108$$
$$108 + 10 = 118$$

Page 15

(1) A Puzzling Inscription—The letter E, which, inserted at the proper intervals, makes the inscription read:
PERSEVERE YE PERFECT MEN,
EVER KEEP THESE PRECEPTS TEN.

(2) Dropped-Letter Proverbs
(1) Faint heart never won fair lady.
(2) Birds of a feather flock together.
(3) He who goes a-borrowing goes a-sorrowing.
(4) Take care of the pence, and the pounds will take care of themselves.

(3) A Puzzle With Coins—Lay out nine counters in three rows of three each, so as to form a square. Distribute the remaining three as follows: place one counter on the first of the first row, another on the second of the second row, and the third on the last of the third row.

(4) A Bridge Problem—The three matches are interlaced as shown below, one resting on the brim of each wineglass. The superincumbent weight binds them together, so that they will sustain a fourth wineglass without difficulty.

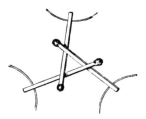

(5) A Square Puzzle—Take away the matches forming the inner sides of the four corner squares. You will have left two squares only, the one in the center of the other.

Page 16

(1) Six Into Three—Take away two matches forming each of the lower corners, and the center match from the top row. This will leave three squares.

(2) Six Into Two—Take away the four matches forming the inner sides of the four squares to the left and the two matches forming the

outer sides of the lower square to the right. You will then have only two squares left, a larger and a smaller.

(3) Five Into Three—First take away the three matches which form the outer sides of the upper left-hand square. Next, remove the two matches forming the outer sides of the upper right-hand square and the two matches forming the outer sides of the lower left-hand square. You have then left two squares, lying diagonally. With four of the matches you removed, form a third square in continuation of the diagonal line.

(4) The Balanced Pencil—You have merely to dig the blade of a half-open penknife in the pencil, a little above the point, and to open or close the blade, little by little, till you find that the balance is obtained. The precise angle must be ascertained by experiment, as it will vary with the length and weight of the two articles. When you have discovered it, the pencil may be balanced, as shown in the figure.

(5) The Cut Playing Card—Fold the card down the center, and cut through the line thus made to within a quarter of an inch of each end. The card will then be as Fig. a. Next, with a sharp penknife or scissors, cut through both thicknesses, alternately to right and left, but each time stopping within a quarter of an inch of the edge, as in Fig. b. The cuts should be about an eighth of an inch apart. The card when opened will be as Fig. c. Open it out still further, when it will form an endless strip, of such a size as to pass easily over a person's body.

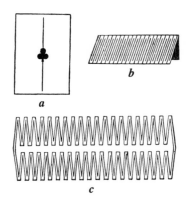

(6) The Balanced Quarter—The first step is to bend the paper clip into the form shown in Fig. a. Use the narrow loop of this as a clip to

56

hold the quarter, bending the wire closer and closer till you have the coin secure. Hang the ring on the hook at the opposite end of the wire, and then proceed to balance it as shown in our illustration. A good many trials will probably be necessary before you are able to ascertain the precise point to which to apply the pin; but, this once found, you may even set the coin spinning (by gently blowing upon the ring) without destroying its equilibrium.

(7) Water Bewitched—Fill a wineglass with water to the brim. Lay a card flat upon it, and turn it over, keeping the card meanwhile in place with the hand. When the glass is inverted the card will not fall when the hand is removed, neither will the water run out, being kept in position by atmospheric pressure. Place the glass thus inverted on a smooth wooden table, near the edge, and cautiously draw away the card. The water will still not run out so long as the glass is not moved, but the moment anyone lifts it the whole will be spilt.

Page 17

(1) Passing The Gate—He had at the outset 61 cents. On the first day he paid a penny at the gate, spent 30 cents, and paid a penny on going out, leaving him with 29 cents. The second day he paid a penny on entering, spent fourteen cents, and after paying a penny on going out was left with 13 cents. The third day he brought in 12 cents, spent 6 cents, and was left on going out with 5 cents. The fourth day he brought in 4 cents, spent 2 cents, and after paying the toll to go out he was left with only 1 penny.

To solve the problem, the calculation must be worked backwards. Thus, on the fourth day he paid a penny on coming out and still had one left, together making 2 cents. He had spent *half* his available money in the town. The total must therefore on that day have been 4 cents, exclusive of the penny he paid to come in. This gives us 5 cents as the amount with which he came out the previous evening. The penny he paid to get out brings this amount to 6 cents, and as he had first spent a like amount, he must previously have had 12 cents, exclusive of the penny to come in. By continuing the same process, it is easy to arrive at his original capital.

(2) A Feat Of Divination—All that is necessary is to deduct 25 from the final sum named. This will give a remainder of two figures, representing the points of the two dice.

Thus, suppose that the points thrown are 6 and 1, and that the thrower selects the former to be multiplied. The figures will then be as follows:
$$(6 \times 2 + 5) \times 5 + 1 = 86$$
$$86 - 25 = 61$$
which, as will be seen, corresponds with the points of the two dice.

If the thrower had selected the 1 as the starting point of the process, the only difference in the result would be that the two digits would come out in reverse order. Thus:

$$(1 \times 2 + 5) \times 5 + 6 = 41$$
$$41 - 25 = 16$$

The same process, in a slightly modified form, is equally applicable to three dice. In this case the steps are as follows:

Multiply the points of the first die by 2; add 5; multiply the result by 5; add the points of the second die; multiply the total by 10; add the points of the third die.

On the final result being announced, the operator subtracts from it 250, when the remainder will give the points of the three dice.

Thus, suppose the points of the three dice to be 5, 4, and 2. Then $5 \times 2 + 5 = 15$; $15 \times 5 = 75$; $75 + 4 = 79$; $79 \times 10 = 790$; $790 + 2 = 792$. And $792 - 250 = 542$, giving the three numbers required.

(3) Hidden Proverbs—The five proverbs are as follows:
A rolling stone gathers no moss.
Too many cooks spoil the broth.
A live dog is more to be feared than a dead lion.
You cannot eat your cake and have it.
Peace hath her victories, no less renowned than war.

To read them, first find the central letter, which is A. This begins the first proverb. Immediately below this will be found R, to the left of this O, and above the O two L's. To the right of the last L are the letters I N. The G, completing the word "rolling," comes next below the N, and below this, S, the initial of the next word, "stone." From the S, moving to the left, we have the remaining letters, T O N E, and so we read on, following the course of the sun, round each square of letters in succession.

For greater clearness we exhibit separately the central square and a few letters of the next square, showing the commencement of the process.

```
    L  I     N
    L  A     G
    O  R     S
E   N  O     T
```

Page 18

(1) The "Forty-Five" Puzzle—The first of the required numbers is 8.
(8 + 2 = 10)
The second is 12. (12 − 2 = 10)
The third is 5.   (5 × 2 = 10)
The fourth is 20. (20 ÷ 2 = 10)
8 + 12 + 5 + 20 = 45.

(2) Squares, Product, & Difference—Answer: 11 and 15. Their product is 165, and their difference is 4. The former exceeds the latter by 161, the sum of their squares is 346, and $346 - 165 = 181$.

(3) The Two Ages—The father was three times the age of his son 15½ years earlier, being then 55½, while his son was 18½. The son will have reached half his father's age in three years' time, being then 37, while his father will be 74.

(4) The Shepherd and His Sheep—To ascertain the number of the flock, find in the first place the least common multiple of 2, 3, 4, 5, and 6, i.e., 60. Then take the lowest multiple of this, which, with 1 added, will be divisible by 7. This will be found to be 301, which is the required answer.

(5) When Will They Get It?—In 420 days; 420 being the least common multiple of 1, 2, 3, 4, 5, 6 and 7.

(6) The Two Sons—The younger son is 24½; the elder, 29¾ years old. The solution is most easily got at by means of a simple equation, thus: Let y = age of younger. Then 5¼y = age of elder. By the terms of the question—
$$5y + 6(y + 5\tfrac{1}{4}) = 301$$
$$5y + 6y + 31\tfrac{1}{2} = 301$$
$$11y = 301 - 31\tfrac{1}{2} = 269\tfrac{1}{2}$$
$$y = 24\tfrac{1}{2}$$
The younger son is therefore 24½ years old, and the elder 24½ + 5¼ = 29¾.

Page 19

The Thirty-Six Puzzle—The six counters are so removed as to leave the remainder shown here.

Page 21

(1) No Two In The Same Row

KS	QD	JC	AH
QC	KH	AS	JD
JH	AC	KD	QS
AD	JS	QH	KC

(2) Things Are Looking Up!—Consider the cards as being numbered 1, 2, and 3. On the first move turn over cards 2 and 3. On the second move turn over cards 1 and 3, and on the third move turn over cards 2 and 3.

(3) The Five Pairs Puzzle—Consider the cards as being numbered from left to right, 1 through 10. The moves would then be: Card 4 on card 1; card 6 on 9; card 8 on 3; card 2 on 7; and card 5 on 10.

Page 22

(1) The Rum Riddle—Any four-legged table or chair.

(2) A Square Deal For Mr. Bang

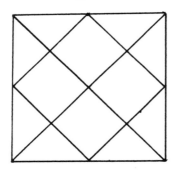

Page 25

A-7, B-19, C-8, D-13, E-20, F-1, G-26, H-21, I-2, J-17, K-25, L-5, M-9, N-23, O-4, P-24, Q-10, R-3, S-22, T-11, U-6, V-15, W-18, X-16, Y-14, Z-12.

Page 27

(1) The Chicken-man

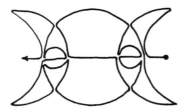

(2) The Surveyors Puzzle—Draw a straight line from point <u>a</u> to point <u>d</u>. Point <u>d</u> is the midpoint of the line <u>c-e</u>. This gives us the triangle <u>a-b-d</u>, which is half of the rectangle made up of side <u>ab</u> and side <u>bd</u>.

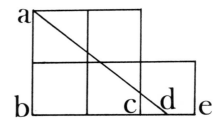

Pages 28 & 29

(1) Defying Gravity—Pick up the bottle, holding the sides near the bottom. Slowly rotate the bottle until the marble is spinning around on the inside. Turn the bottle mouth downward and walk toward the other table. Centrifugal force will keep the marble from falling out. At all times you must keep rotating the bottle as you move across the room. Once you have reached the other table, turn the bottle mouth upward and place it upon the table.

(2) Paper Bridge—All you have to do is to pleat the paper and the puzzle is solved (Fig. 1). **(3) A Loopy Problem**—Place your forefinger inside the loop and give the loop a quick sidewise blow. It must be a sharp blow and you must follow through sweeping the loop out from under the dime. The dime will then fall straight down and into the bottle. **(4) Chug-A-Mug**—Before you cut the string you must first take a loop of string about two feet above the mug and tie a knot in it (Fig. 2). You can now cut the string (the part that makes up the loop) and the knot will keep the mug from falling to the floor.

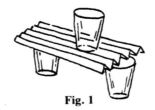

Fig. 1   **Fig. 2**

Page 30

(1) S̲T̲R̲I̲K̲E̲ W̲H̲I̲L̲E̲ T̲H̲E̲ I̲R̲O̲N̲'S̲ H̲O̲T̲

(2) Step 1: $20'' \times 4 = 80''$ circumference

Step 2: $\dfrac{80}{3.14} = 25.48$ diameter

Step 3: $25.48 \times 25.48 = 649.23$ area of square

Step 4: $\dfrac{25.48}{2} = 12.74$ radius of circle

Step 5: $12.74 \times 12.74 \times 3.14 = 509.65$ area of circle

Step 6: $\begin{array}{r} 649.23 \\ \underline{509.65} \\ 139.58 \end{array}$ = area of corners

Step 7: $\dfrac{139.58}{4} = 34.9$ square inches area of spider's web.

(3) Answer: $5.25. Take the section with three links and the section with four links and have all seven links opened. These seven links can now be used to join the other seven sections together. **(4)** It can be done in just four moves. Jump 5 over 8, 9, 3, 1. Jump 7 over 4. Jump 6 over 2, 7. Jump 5 over 6, which leaves the last checker in the middle. **(5)** Answer: June 4, 1976 at 12:00 noon. For the three clocks to again show 12:00 at the same time it is necessary for the first clock to lose twelve hours and for the second clock to gain twelve hours.

This will take exactly 720 days. Add this to June 15, 1974 and we get June 4, 1976 (1976 was a leap year).

Pages 36 & 37

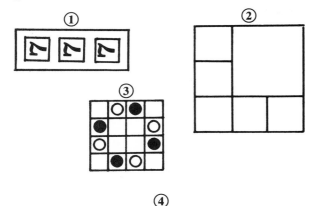

If B had seen two gray helmets he would have known that he was wearing a white helmet, and have said so. Since B had said nothing C knew that he couldn't have a gray helmet on, so C declared first, giving Merlin the reason why he could not be wearing a white helmet.

Page 39

(1) A lawsuit. (2) Mustard. (3) The one with the largest head. (4) A yardstick. (5) Because it is planted in the spring. (6) The stone would get wet. (7) A barber has razors to shave and a mother has shavers to raise. (8) Sunday. The rest are weekdays. (9) Music.

Page 40

(1) **Transposition**—2 to 1, 6 to 2, 4 to 6, 7 to 4, 3 to 7, 5 to 3, 1 to 5.

(2) **Captain Kidd's Kite Puzzle**

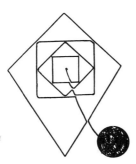

Page 42

(1)	(2)	(3)
8384	98765	
803	1234	
626	99,999	
50		
8		
9871		

$$\sqrt{I} = I$$

Page 45

The secret move that the red forces must make before they can capture the monster is to ignore the black piece and move out directly towards position 1. Entering position 1 by way of position 3 and

leaving by 2, or entering by 2 and leaving by 3, bestows upon the red side the power to defeat the powers of darkness. Your opening moves, disregarding what moves black may make, should be: 26-24, 24-20, 20-19, 19-15, 15-11, 11-7, 7-3, 3-1, 1-2. After making the last move, it is time for the red forces to go on the attack. Pursue the black piece, pushing him always away from position 1 in the northwest corner. It will only be a matter of time before you capture the enemy. If he gets around you and manages to pass through position 1 you will have to return and go through position 1 to regain your advantage. One last puzzle: see if you can analyze this game and come up with the reason that makes position 1 so important in delivering certain victory to the red side.

Page 47

Tintinnabulation—Fold the large link (b), as in Fig. 1, and slip the small link over the end marked d. Now, hang the bell on the link as shown in Fig. 1 and slip the small link back over end d and down onto the bell. Open up the large link and the puzzle is made (Fig. 2). When you fold the large link just bend it, do not crease it, so that when you open it out there will be no indication that it was ever folded.

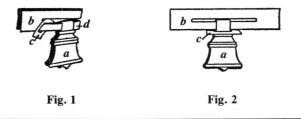

Fig. 1   **Fig. 2**

Page 48

The four dotted lines in the diagram below are the lines that the "Steam Man" had to go over twice. His route was A to D, D to C and back to D, D to G, G to H and back, G to B, B to E and back, B to F, F to J and back, and F to K.

Page 49

(1) **The Golf Puzzle**—The two shots that Dashing Dan plays are a 150-yard drive and a 125-yard approach shot. The holes are made in the following manner: 150 yards: 1 drive; 300 yards: 2 drives; 250 yards: 2 approaches; 325 yards: 3 drives, 1 approach back; 275 yards: 1 drive, 1 approach; 350 yards: 4 approaches, 1 drive back; 225 yards: 3 approaches, 1 drive back; 400 yards: 1 drive, 2 approaches; 425 yards: 2 drives, 1 approach. (2) **The Archery Range**—The Hood sisters put 2 arrows in the 25 circle, 2 arrows in the 20 circle, and 2 arrows in the 3 circle.

Page 51

A sure way to win is to go first and play a five. If the other player plays a five, you play a two. If he again plays a five, you again play a two. If he then plays the last five, you again play a two. If at any time your opponent does not play a five, you will be able to make a 10, 17, 24, or 31 and win.